# DOWNTOWN ST. LOUIS

**NINI HARRIS**

Foreword by Charlie Brennan

Photo edited by
Don Korte

Copyright © 2015, Reedy Press, LLC
All rights reserved.

Reedy Press
PO Box 5131
St. Louis, MO 63139
www.reedypress.com

No part of this publication may be reproduced or transmitted in any form or by any means, electronic or mechanical, including photocopy, recording, or any information storage and retrieval system, without permission in writing from the publisher.

Permissions may be sought directly from Reedy Press at the above mailing address or via our website at www.reedypress.com.

Cover Design: Jill Halpin
Book Design: Jill Halpin and Julie Sturma

Library of Congress Control Number: 2015942719

ISBN: 9781681060156

Printed in the United States
15 16 17 18 19  5 4 3 2 1

# TABLE OF CONTENTS

| | |
|---|---|
| Acknowledgments | IV |
| Foreword | VII |
| Introduction | 1 |
| Chapter 1: 1764–1816 | 11 |
| Chapter 2: 1817–1873 | 29 |
| Chapter 3: 1874–1916 | 49 |
| Chapter 4: 1917–1945 | 83 |
| Chapter 5: 1945–Present | 113 |
| Endnotes | 144 |
| Photo Credits | 147 |
| Index | 148 |

# ACKNOWLEDGMENTS

*The following individuals helped locate and access historical materials:*

St. Louis Public Library staff members: Cynthia Millar, Kyle Criner, Nancy Oliver, and Tom Pearson in the Genealogy Room; Adele Heagney and Kirwin Roach in the St. Louis Room; Renee Jones in Special Collections; Louise Powderly in the History Room; and Bill Olbrich in the Business, Government & Law Room.

*The Campbell House Museum staff members:*

Andrew Hahn, executive director; Thomas Gronski, board member and volunteer researcher; and David Newmann, weekend manager.

*The Eugene Field House staff members:*

Kimberly Ann Larson, director; and Stephanie Bliss, assistant director.

*Jefferson National Parks Association staff:*

Jennifer R. Clark, C.A., archivist; Thomas Dewey, librarian; and Kathleen Moenster, assistant curator.

Bette Constantin, Jay Unnerstall, and Vincent C. Schoemehl Jr., mayor, city of St. Louis, 1981–1993.

Editorial input was provided by Bob Moore, historian, Jefferson National Expansion Memorial, and by Kathy Kaznell, without whom this book would not have been possible.

*The following individuals assisted with locating historical images or access for current photography:*

Baileys' Range—Jim Bailey

City Museum—Rick Erwin

CityArchRiver Project—Ryan McClure and Tom Nagel

Civil Courts and Carnahan Courthouse—Thom Gross

Culinaria—Paul Simon, Scott Wilmoth, and Adam Scheer (Schnucks/Culinaria)

Flying Saucer Draught Emporium—Larry Richardson (8.0 Management)

Missouri Athletic Club—Jim Wilson

Missouri History Museum—Molly Kodner and Dennis Northcott

Old Post Office—Eliza Holman (The Desco Group)

Saint Louis Carriage Company

St. Louis Public Library—Gerald Brooks

"Street illuminations" were installed for festivals and celebrations. This illumination, installed in the fall of 1892, featured portraits of American presidents.

# FOREWORD

by Charlie Brennan

Downtown St. Louis could be the older brother of the United States as the two were born about twelve years apart. But in schools, the older sibling gets neglected; students from St. Louis study their country quite a bit more than they study their city.

As a result, with the exception of beer and baseball, too little of downtown's history is known by the adults who inhabit it every day.

That's a shame because downtown St. Louis, as Nini Harris demonstrates in this book, has a fascinating past. A president, Ulysses Grant, got married here. Great writers like Tennessee Williams worked here. International figures like Lafayette and Dickens visited here. Top architects like Louis Sullivan created influential buildings here.

Now, thanks to Harris, we learn the stories behind the buildings we work in, the sidewalks we walk on, and the statues we pass. These stories change the way we look at Olive Street, the riverfront, Union Station, the Eads Bridge, etc.

I'm convinced as we learn more about downtown St. Louis, we'll develop a greater appreciation of this part of our region. In turn, we'll retell Harris's stories again and again, and by doing so, enhance the "esprit de corps," as Chouteau might have called it, for the city he founded.

If you didn't learn about downtown St. Louis in your classroom, don't worry. NiNi Harris, like the mounted King Louis IX, is charging to the rescue.

Early movie houses like the Strand and Columbia Theaters on Sixth Street entertained St. Louisans with silent movies accompanied by live music.

# INTRODUCTION

The skyline of downtown St. Louis, framed and focused by the Gateway Arch, is instantly recognizable to people from around the globe. The graceful Arch is not only an icon for all of St. Louis, but its very shape also symbolizes the city's role in American history as the Gateway to the West. And its simple elegance also reflects the optimism of the space age.

Downtown St. Louis at twilight.

Downtown St. Louis, however, is more than its striking skyline. The real estate stretching from the banks of the Mississippi west to Jefferson Avenue and from Dr. Martin Luther King Boulevard south to Chouteau Avenue has been the core, the heart, and the soul of St. Louis since French merchants chose the site to establish a fur trade with the Indians in 1764.

In what became downtown St. Louis, these French frontiersmen built homes of log and stone. They farmed maize and herded cattle, and they eventually built flour mills, planing mills, and blacksmith shops. With the coming of steam power, paddle wheelers carried thousands of emigrants from the Eastern states and all over Europe to the riverbanks of St. Louis. Explorers, military expeditions, commercial ventures, and settlers looking for a new home in the vast American West all began their journey in downtown St. Louis.

During the Civil War, downtown St. Louis became a staging area for the Union army and also provided hospitals for the thousands of wounded who were brought upriver from the Battle of Shiloh and the Siege of Vicksburg.

Following the Civil War, factories produced the grease for the wagon wheels, the cast-iron

A hodgepodge of advertising cluttered the corner of Twelfth and Market Streets at the turn of the century. Scenes like this encouraged the development of Memorial Plaza, a ribbon of parkway through the core of downtown.

Immigrants working in St. Louis foundries manufactured cast-iron stoves, like this one produced by Bridge, Beach & Company.

stoves for the ranch hands' bunkhouses, the brooms pioneer women used to sweep out sod houses, and the shoes worn by the townspeople going to church.

These factories and warehouses not only supplied the American West, but in World War I and World War II, these energetic businesses and workers also produced and shipped supplies needed for the American armies to be victorious.

While being the Gateway to the West and providing the nation with economic muscle, St. Louisans created a lasting gift. They constructed every office building,

The ceiling of the Law Library in the top floors of the Civil Courts Building was inspired by Renaissance-era design. The Law Library Association was incorporated in 1839. In 1930, the library moved into its current space, which was designed for it, in the Civil Courts Building.

Lush terra-cotta featuring unique designs trimmed Louis Sullivan's Wainwright Building.

The arrival of horseless carriages on the streets of downtown St. Louis began a radical transformation in how downtown functioned.

store, or warehouse to be a thing of beauty. They imbued this great architecture with the quality of materials and craftsmanship that gave it permanence. The St. Louis Public Library's Central Branch, like many of downtown's great structures, was inspired by the great architecture of Europe. Other buildings, most notably Louis Sullivan's Wainwright Building, represented innovative ways of building.

    This extraordinary downtown, filled with magnificent architecture and built to stand for

The Old Post Office is a commanding building, designed to be admired from every angle. When the building opened in 1884, it housed the post office, the custom house, the federal courthouse, the collector of internal revenue, lighthouse and steamboat inspectors, and the Army Corps of Engineers. It was one of only three sub-treasuries in the entire country.

generations, stirs many family memories. Family stories are tied to downtown by the ancestor who worked at the Majestic Stove Factory on Twentieth Street or by the great-grandfather who arrived at Union Station to build a new life in America. For some, the story of the grandmother who did piecework in the Fashion Square Building on Washington Avenue or the uncle who enlisted in the

Architect Edward Durell Stone incorporated arches sculpted out of thin concrete shells into his design for Busch Stadium. This photo was taken on July 8, 1966, during a game between the Cardinals and the Houston Astros.

Streetlight on Laclede's Landing.

U.S. Army at the Federal Building the day after the Japanese attack on Pearl Harbor connects them to downtown. The memory of camping out on the sidewalk at the old Busch Stadium to get a bleacher ticket for a World Series game or shivering in a brisk March wind while cheering a band in the St. Patrick's Day parade—these memories make St. Louisans smile.

All this history and the memories connected with downtown—a downtown that awes visitors with its architectural jewels and symbolized by the phenomenal Gateway Arch—make downtown the core, the heart, and the soul of St. Louis.

After its dedication in 1938, Soldiers' Memorial became the setting for patriotic celebrations.

The founding of St. Louis was romanticized in this painting of Pierre Laclede and Auguste Chouteau landing at the site of St. Louis in 1764. A Native American in elaborate headdress ceremoniously waits on the riverbank in this work painted by August Becker after Carl Wimar's original painting in the Old Courthouse.

## Chapter 1

# 1764–1816

*As a teenager, Auguste Chouteau assisted his stepfather with the establishment of St. Louis. Late in his life, Chouteau wrote an account of the founding of St. Louis when it was a bustling metropolis of the West. Excerpts from this narrative follow.*

"Laclede was delighted to see the location (where St. Louis is now). He did not hesitate a moment to make the settlement there he envisioned. Besides the beauty of the site, he found there all the advantages one could desire in founding a settlement that might later become very large. After thoroughly inspecting everything, he decided on the place where he wished to make his settlement, notched some trees with his own hand, and said: "Chouteau, come here as soon as navigation opens. Have this place cleared to make our settlement, after the plan I shall give you. . . .

"I arrived at the designated place on the 15th of (February) in the morning. The next day I put the men to work. They began the storehouse, which was built in a short time, and the little cabins.

"Around the early part of April, Laclede arrived among us. He looked after his settlement, determined the place where he wanted to build his house, [and] made a plan of the village, which he named St. Louis in honor of [King] Louis XV, whose subject he expected to remain for a long time."[1]

A portrait of Pierre Laclede, the French merchant and military veteran who founded the outpost of St. Louis in 1764.

A portrait of Auguste Chouteau, who at age thirteen assisted his stepfather Pierre Laclede with the founding of St. Louis.

The first residents of downtown St. Louis lived in houses built with upright logs that were surrounded by gallery-style porches. In their yards framed with wood stockades or picket fences, they grew vegetable and herb gardens and kept chickens. Muddy streets separated the rectangular blocks of their village, which hugged the Mississippi River. From Fourth Street all the way to Jefferson Avenue, these first residents of downtown cultivated fields of wheat and Indian maize. They stored furs and pelts harvested in the north, and they stored the manufactured goods needed for trade with the Indians. They attended mass in a small, wooden church, and after 1770 their village officially served as a colonial capital city. For the first half century of the city of St. Louis, all of St. Louis was within what became downtown. It began as a French village, loosely governed by the Spanish colonial empire and dependent on trade with the Osage Indians.

French merchant and military veteran Pierre Laclede, assisted by his thirteen-year-old stepson, Auguste Chouteau, had founded the outpost on limestone terraces along the Mississippi in 1764. As St. Louis grew, it clung to the riverbank, because the Mississippi River was the village's lifeblood. It connected the village to the profitable fur trade to the north and west, and it was the highway to New Orleans.

The line of communication for this frontier outpost was precarious—twelve hundred river miles between St. Louis and New Orleans. In the spring, men loaded boats with furs and pelts and then headed south on the river. Spring floods sometimes made that trip, which required a few weeks to a month, perilous. After emptying their

Flatboatmen, in their primitive craft, kept young St. Louis connected with other settlements in the Creole corridor and with the market for furs in New Orleans. This hand-colored wood engraving depicts the rugged crew relaxing on the comparatively easy trip downriver.

*French military engineer Nicolas de Finiels, who stayed in St. Louis during 1797–98, described the livestock and produce raised in what is now downtown.*

"They own 1,200 to 1,500 head of cattle and nearly 250 horses; harvest 5,000 to 6,000 bushels of wheat, 5,000 of maize, and 2,000 pounds of tobacco; and produce oats and hay for fodder. They cultivate all varieties of vegetables and several European fruits—apples, pears, peaches, grapes, tart cherries, and currants. In the woods not far from town you can find hazelnuts, wild cherries, persimmons, pawpaws, pecans, wild grapes, blackberries, mulberries, and American walnuts. . . . Wild strawberries abound in the fields and woods."[2]

While sketching and painting watercolors, early St. Louisan Anna Maria Von Phul (1786–1823) recorded what downtown St. Louis looked like during the Spanish colonial and American territorial days.

*De Finiels commented on St. Louis's improved quality of life after the arrival of some Americans.*

"St. Louis was given a boost when some Americans settled in the area six years ago. . . . Sawmills now supply abundant planks at twenty-five sous apiece. . . . Iron is available at a better price; masonry, cabinetry, carpentry, and furniture are less expensive. . . . Vegetables, eggs, poultry, milk, butter, and grain are more readily available, and thanks to the Americans' industry subsistence is generally more secure than before."[3]

boats in New Orleans, they loaded keelboats with tons of manufactured goods. To power the boats up the treacherous river, the flatboatmen had only their own muscle. Much of the way upstream they poled the boats, pushing long poles into the river bottom and propelling the boats forward against the current. Where the riverbank provided a path, the boatmen walked along that bank, pulling the boats upriver with heavy ropes over their shoulders.

The boats were piled high with knives, guns, traps, cloth, pottery, glass, pots, rope, canvas—anything that could not be handmade from raw materials in a frontier outpost.

Laclede invited Creoles and Frenchmen living on the east side of the river to resettle in St. Louis.

Illinois had been ceded to the English after their victory in the French and Indian War. Though it was announced in 1764 that the French had ceded the west side of the river (including the site of St. Louis) to Spain, many Frenchmen of Illinois still came to St. Louis. They preferred the government of the distant Spanish colonial empire to that of their ancestral enemy, the English. Farmers came to St. Louis from Fort de Chartres, Cahokia, and St. Philippe.

As soon as their homes were built in the new village, these first residents of downtown St. Louis began to till the soil. They cultivated the common fields west of Fourth Street that were divided into long narrow strips, later the footprint of many of downtown's east-west streets. Out of season, they worked as artisans, blacksmiths, carpenters, stonemasons, and hewers. Some spent the winters trading with Indians and trapping, harvesting a valuable stock of furs.

A small influx of new French immigrants who were fleeing the violent aftermath of the French Revolution boosted the population in the 1790s. After visiting the area's French settlements and St. Louis in 1797–98, a French engineer noted that "everyone is more or less an urbanite and a peasant at the same time. City habits begin where plowing and hunting leave off, and the morning farmer is sometimes the evening dandy, striving to be socially adept."[4]

The document transferring Upper Louisiana to the United States, dated 1804, bears official waxed seals.

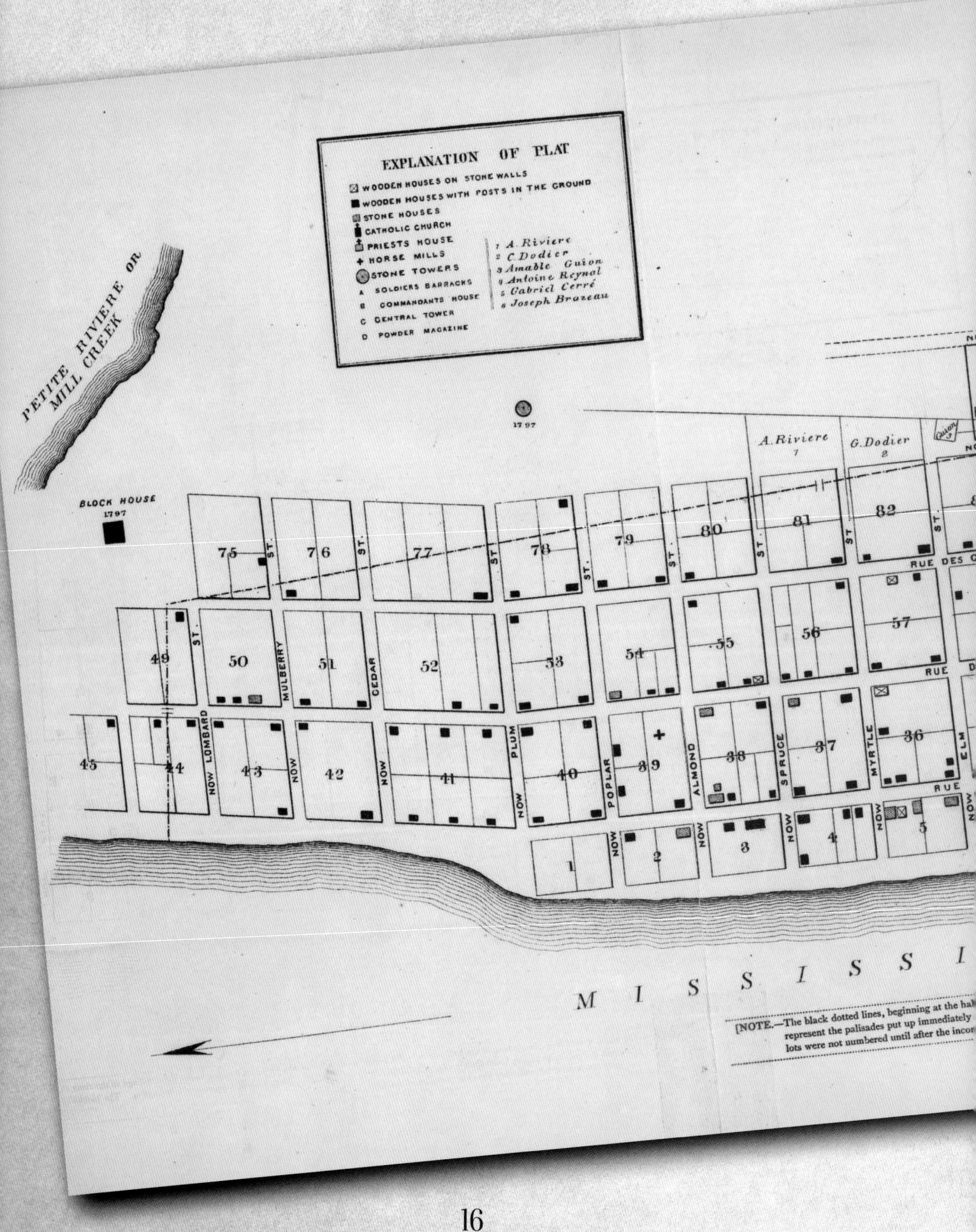

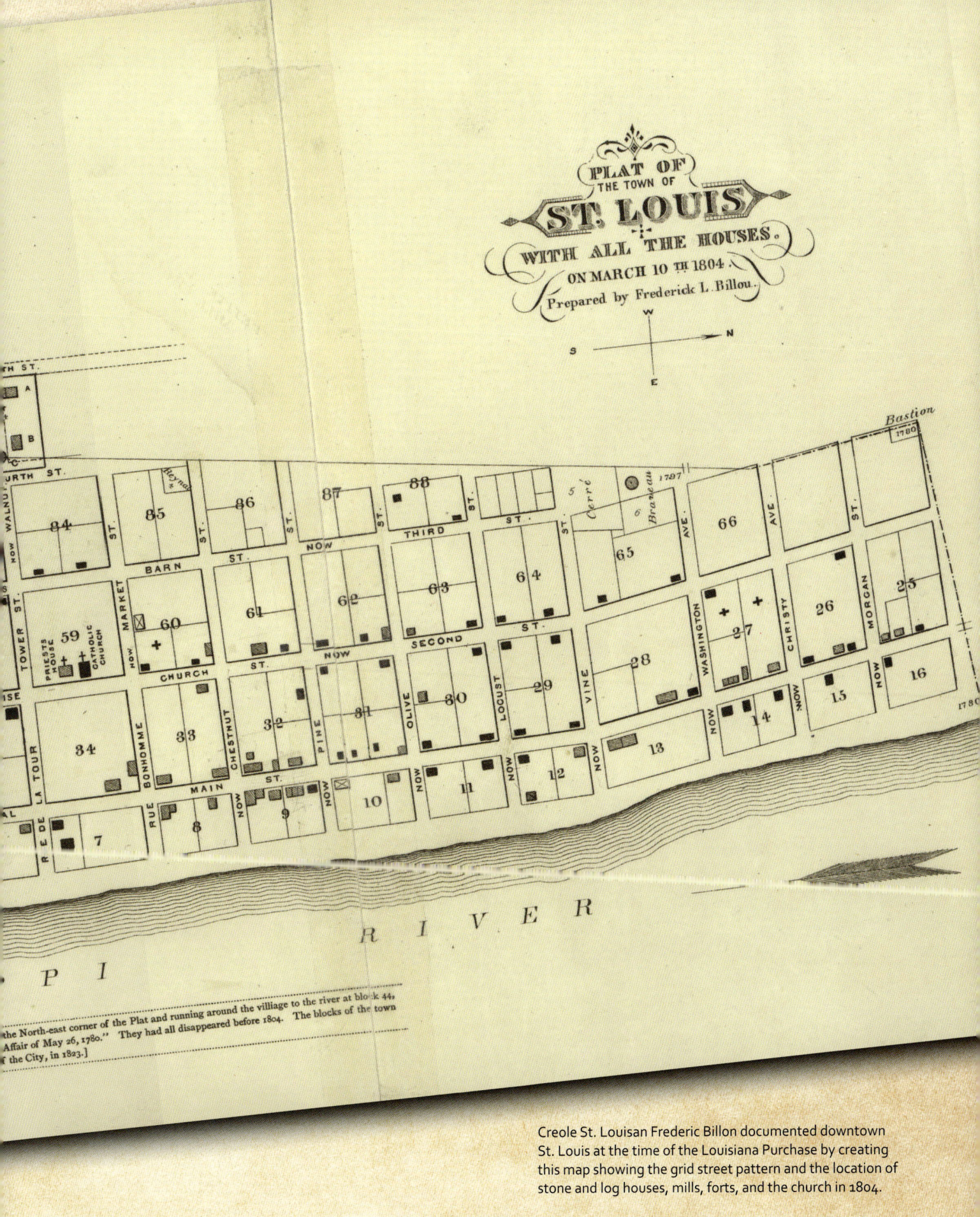

Creole St. Louisan Frederic Billon documented downtown St. Louis at the time of the Louisiana Purchase by creating this map showing the grid street pattern and the location of stone and log houses, mills, forts, and the church in 1804.

The Beaugenou family, among St. Louis's earliest settlers, built their home on Third Street in Creole style with a hipped roof and using logs set upright. A sheltering gallery stretched thirty-five feet along the length of the house.

The home of Dr. Antoine Saugrain, a French-born descendent of booksellers, boasted the finest flower garden in St. Louis. It was located on Second Street just south of the present-day Arch grounds.

In 1804 President Thomas Jefferson's Louisiana Purchase more than doubled the territory of the young United States of America. This "biggest real estate deal in history" turned the French outpost of St. Louis into American territory. When St. Louis was transferred to the United States as part of the Louisiana Purchase, the village had a distinctly French colonial appearance.

About four-fifths of the houses were French-style log cabins, with the logs set upright in a trench about three or four feet into the ground. Some were of round posts, others were hand-hewn logs about nine inches square. The French colonials used mud mixed with straw as mortar or bousillage between the posts. The walls were often whitewashed. The more prosperous villagers built their log

Chouteau's mill, at Eighth and Spruce Streets, created Chouteau's Pond by damming La Petite Riviere that flowed around the southern edge of downtown. By the time this photo was taken, the mill was used as a stone saw mill.

In 1797, Antoine Roy petitioned the Spanish governor for a six-hundred-square-foot tract at Biddle Street on the riverfront to build this windmill. For decades a landmark on the north riverfront, the abandoned stone windmill has been mistakenly identified as a Spanish fort. Early photographer Emil Boehl took this photo with the steamer *Wyoming* at the riverbank.

homes with high stone ground floors. That ground floor was often used for storage or a kitchen. The poorest homes had a gallery or porch along one wall, while the largest had galleries all around.

The village was framed on the south by Mill Creek, originally called La Petite Riviere. It flowed from the common fields around the southern edge of the village into the Mississippi. Auguste Chouteau operated a mill (near Eighth and Spruce Streets) that dammed the little river and created a large pond. A stone tower built as a windmill by Antoine Roy framed the northern edge of the village.

After the Louisiana Purchase, the "early Americans" and Irish immigrants began arriving in St. Louis: young American officer Captain Amos Stoddard, who served as the first American commandant of Upper Louisiana; Rufus Easton, who became postmaster; and Irish patriot Joseph Charless, who founded the first newspaper west of the Mississippi. In 1809, St. Louis was incorporated as a town, using Roy's

*In May 1816, missionary Timothy Flint arrived in St. Louis. The Massachusetts native was impressed with the French character of the young St. Louis. In his comments, he noted the Indian mound north of downtown.*

"St. Louis, as you approach it, shows, like all the other French towns in this region, to much the greatest advantage at a distance. The French mode of building, and the white coat of lime applied to the mud or rough stone walls, give them a beauty at a distance, which gives place to their native meanness, when you inspect them from a nearer point of view. The town shows to very great advantage, when seen from the opposite shore, in the American bottom. The site is naturally a most beautiful one, rising gradually from the shore to the summit of the bluff, like an amphitheater. It contains many handsome, and a few splendid buildings. The country about it is an open, pleasant, and undulating kind of half prairie, half shrubbery. A little beyond the town, there is considerable smooth grass prairie. . . . Just beyond the skirts of the town, are some old, white, stone forts, built in Spanish times, as defences against the Indians, which have a romantic and beautiful appearance. A little northeast of the town, you see a mound of a conical form and considerable elevation, an interesting relic of the olden time."[5]

FIRST MARKET HOUSE, 1812. (STONE.)
[Drawn under direction of Fred. L. Billon.]

St. Louis's market house was the first market west of the Mississippi River. It provided twelve stalls and measured sixty-four feet long and thirty feet wide.

PL. 20.

Indian of the Nation of the Kaskaskia

*A few days after he arrived, missionary Timothy Flint observed the arrival of Native Americans for a council in St. Louis. He noted the tribal differences in their watercraft and in the shelters they constructed during their stay.*

"from different points of the upper Mississippi, Missouri, and the lakes, a great number of the principal warriors and chiefs of the tribes of these regions, to attend a grand council with commissioners assembled under the authority of the United States, to make treaties of peace with the tribes that had been hostile to us during the war. Their squaws and children attended them. . . .

"Those from the lakes, and the high points of the Mississippi, had beautiful canoes, or rather large skiffs, of white birch bark. Those from the lower Mississippi, and from the Missouri, had pirogues, or canoes hollowed out of a large tree. Some tribes covered their tents with bear-skins. Those from far up the Mississippi, had beautiful cone-shaped tents, made very neatly with rush matting."[6]

AM OBERN MISSOURI
EIN DORF DER MANDAN-INDIANER.

The Upper Missouri
A Mandan Indian Village

Tower (the stone windmill) as the beginning of the town limits on the north side. The entire town was within what is now downtown St. Louis.

In May 1816, the first subdivision west of the old French village limits opened. The subdivision "on the hill" extended from Fourth Street west to Seventh Street and from Spruce to St. Charles Street. Gradually, the more prosperous residents started building grander homes in this district, away from the growing commerce and traffic along the river. At the core of this subdivision was a new, American-style public square that would be the site of the courthouse.

The town's growing wealth and sophistication did not, however, end its extreme isolation. Whether French, Creole, African, or "early American," these St. Louisans were connected to the rest of the continent by men who used their own muscle to power the boats and supplies upstream.

Steam power would change everything.

Watercolor painted by Anna Maria Von Phul in 1818 documents the Big Mound in the landscape of early St. Louis.

a.

b.

c.

a. A WPA mural of the flatboatmen in the post office at 1800 Market Street.
b. Auguste Chouteau's residence.
c. Statue of Pierre Laclede on Market Street next to city hall.
d. Anna Maria Von Phul watercolor of woman and boy in Creole dress.
e. Thomas Easterly daguerreotype from 1854 showing Chouteau's Pond after it was drained.
f. A postcard of Creole ruins on the riverfront postmarked 1909.

Four- and five-story commercial buildings with cast-iron and stone ornament were replacing townhouses when this photo was taken in 1872 looking west on Olive Street from Fourth Street.

## Chapter 2

# 1817–1873

In November 1818, John Darby and his household arrived in St. Louis. They traveled by land from North Carolina with a large covered wagon and a two-wheeled carriage. His son, also named John Darby, served several terms as mayor of St. Louis beginning in 1835. Years later, Mayor Darby described St. Louis as it appeared in 1818, when two-thirds of the inhabitants were French speaking.

"When we reached the eastern bank of the Mississippi, and saw for the first time the town of St. Louis, it had even then a striking and imposing appearance when viewed from the opposite shore. . . ."[7]

"Main Street was pretty compactly built, mostly with stone, though some frame and log houses still existed, the log houses of the French being, however, different from those built by the Americans. The French built by hewing the logs, and then planting them in the ground perpendicularly; while the Americans laid the logs horizontally, and notched them together at the corners.

"All the rich people lived on Main Street; all the fine houses were there. All the stores were on Main Street; all the business of the town was transacted there. In the upper part of Second, or Church Street, there were few houses; in the lower part there were more. The houses occupied by families then were generally small; there were a few brick houses in the town, perhaps not more than five or six."[8]

Beginning July 27, 1817, when the steam-powered riverboat *Pike* landed at the levee, the historic core of St. Louis evolved from a frontier river town into the energetic downtown of a major industrialized American city. Steam-powered river traffic fueled St. Louis's burgeoning economy, making it a powerful transportation hub, then spurring its industrial development. With paddle wheelers feeding commerce and bringing new workers and citizens, the city grew from fewer than five thousand residents to more than three hundred thousand. Physically, the town expanded from 385 acres to almost 18 square miles. By 1874, the old town was filled with packed warehouses, bustling hotels, churches with towering steeples, tenements, comfortable residential areas, and factories. Sprawling ethnic neighborhoods were spreading to the south and north of downtown, with new arrivals from Germany, Bohemia, and Ireland filling the streets of these neighborhoods. The speed that steam power offered was the catalyst of this booming development.

During St. Louis's first half century, only the sturdiest of settlers could make the trip to the city. The three months by boat, against the strong current, upriver from New Orleans was exhausting. Compared with the rigors of traveling by keelboat, the two-week steamboat trip, arduous by today's standards, was luxurious. Signs of urban development appeared soon after the coming of steam-powered boats.

The first street was paved, the first sidewalk paved, and the Wiggins Ferry Company acquired exclusive rights to operate ferry services at St. Louis by 1822. Twice each day the ferry traveled from the foot of Market Street to Morgan Street, which was their second landing place, and then to the opposite bank. Only four years after the *Pike* arrived,

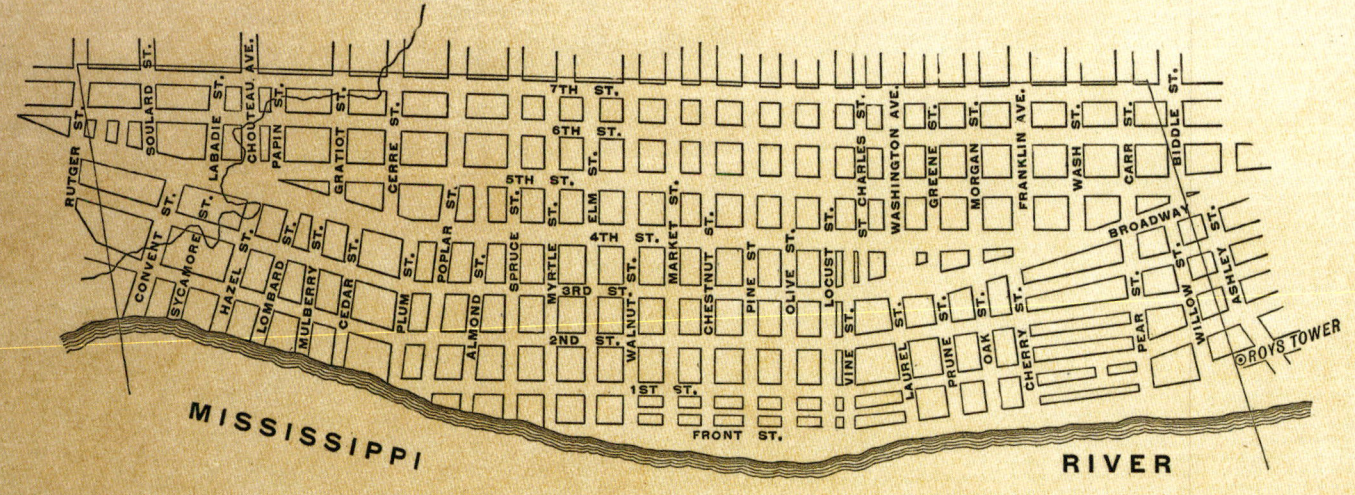

Boundary of 1822.    Act of Legislature, Dec. 9th, 1822.    0.74 Square Miles

Population 5,000

*Jessie Benton Fremont was the daughter of influential Missouri senator Thomas Hart Benton and wife of explorer, Republican candidate for president, and Union general John C. Fremont. As a child, she lived in Washington, D.C., when the Congress was in session but returned to St. Louis in the spring. In her memoirs, she described what is now downtown St. Louis in the 1830s.*

"Coming back to St. Louis always in springtime, even after the mild winters of Washington the contrast was charming. . . . here the tawny swift Mississippi was stirring with busy life, and the little city itself, was animated from its thronged river-bank out through to the Indian camps on the rolling prairie back of the town.

"And it was such an embowered fragrant place in that season; the thickets of wild plum and the wild crab-apples which covered the prairie embalmed the air, and everywhere was the honey-scent of the locust.[9]

"The houses were built in the Creole way; a courtyard surrounded by a four-sided house with broad galleries all round, which sat peacefully in the midst of trees and gardens and orchards on the gentle slope looking to the wide muddy torrent of the Mississippi and the flat green plain beyond of 'the Illinois.'"[10]

Artist A. C. Warren viewed bustling St. Louis from the Illinois riverbank in 1872 for this hand-colored steel engraving. He included a completed Eads Bridge, then under construction, in the background.

St. Louis was incorporated as a city. It included the acreage from the river west to Seventh Street and from Mill Creek on the south to Roy's Tower on the north.

Though the city boasted a growing port, expanding commerce, and municipal government, St. Louis was still a frontier outpost when General Lafayette, hero of the American Revolution, paid a formal visit in 1825. Since the city had no budget for official gatherings, citizens volunteered their resources to conduct dignified ceremonies. But on April 29, as soon as Lafayette disembarked from the riverboat and made a few appropriate remarks, a local butcher named Jacob Roth joined the festivities. He was notorious for stealing cows, butchering them, and then selling the meat to the real owner. Greasy from his work that day, he enthusiastically shouted, "Whooraw for liberty! Old Fellow, just give me your hand. Whooraw for liberty! Hand out your paw old fellow."

He grabbed Lafayette's hand and began shaking it vigorously. A drunken committeeman started shouting, "Go 'way from there, I tell you! You stole a cow." While the thieving greasy butcher and inebriated committeeman made a scene, a carriage was requisitioned to carry Lafayette away. A citizen loaned his personal carriage, the most elegant in town, and a pair of horses to transport Lafayette. Another citizen loaned a second pair of horses. The horses, not used to working together, balked. Finally, the horses pulled Lafayette to Major Pierre Chouteau's elegantly furnished home, where the major hosted the festivities. The bill for entertaining the great Lafayette totaled $37.[11]

Despite early stumbles at ceremony, the city left behind some of its frontier ruggedness. A federal customhouse opened on the riverfront, and the handsome Greek Revival cathedral was dedicated in 1834. Six years later the census counted

A wood engraving from 1840 shows the Old Cathedral, in its original context, with the rectory on the right and orphanage on the left.

16,469 residents of St. Louis, including descendants of the early French. Others had emigrated in equal numbers from New England, the Mid-Atlantic, and Southern states. African Americans included many living enslaved but others living as free persons of color, and within a few years, Germans, Bohemians, and Irish were settling in the city. Many unique figures were among St. Louis's early population. A Spanish buccaneer and several of Jean Lafitte's pirates lived out their days here. Downtown was home to explorer William Clark, who served as the nation's agent for Indian affairs in the West, and a slave named Elizabeth Keckley, who would win her freedom and become a confidante of Mary Todd Lincoln.

Matthew Hastings, who arrived in St. Louis in 1840, documented St. Louis through his artwork. In this painting from 1842, he showed early residences with large yards dating to the Spanish colonial era still scattered amongst the then new multi-story commercial buildings at Third and Olive Streets.

*In 1841 English author Charles Dickens and his wife visited St. Louis as part of a six-month tour of the United States. The couple stayed at the Planter's House, the large hotel at Fourth and Chestnut Streets. Dickens published his travelogue,* American Notes, *in 1842 and gave the Planter's House a glowing review.*

"We went to a large hotel, called the Planter's House: built like an English hospital, with long passages and bare walls, and sky-lights above the room-doors for the free circulation of air. There were a great many boarders in it; and as many lights sparkled and glistened from the windows down into the street below, when we drove up, as if it had been illuminated on some occasion of rejoicing. It is an excellent house, and the proprietors have most bountiful notions of providing the creature comforts. Dining alone with my wife in our own room one day, I counted fourteen dishes on the table at once."[12]

Buildings line Front Street and steamboats line the levee in this painting by John Caspar Wild dating to 1840. People crowd the second-story pavilion of the market house and African Americans and Native Americans are among the people on the riverfront.

Only seven years after Lafayette's visit to rustic St. Louis, Jesuit missionaries gained a university charter for St. Louis University and built dorms, a church, and classrooms on Washington Avenue and Ninth Street. Later, Washington University would be located on Washington Avenue around Seventeenth Street.

Thousands more were passing through St. Louis as the city funneled westward expansion. Many explorers, missionaries, soldiers, miners, and settlers made St. Louis their starting point.

The ordnance used by Fremont's expeditions, the traps used by the mountain men, the saddles and rope used by cattlemen, the coffee brewed over the morning campfire . . . they all came from St. Louis. As the river fed St. Louis, downtown St. Louis fueled the nation's expansion.

For a mile beginning at Biddle Street on the north, paddle wheelers lined the riverfront, nose to the levee. A forest of smokestacks belched white smoke with sparks into the air. The population had multiplied nearly fivefold by 1849, when a moored paddle wheeler caught fire. The fire spread to the adjacent boat. It broke loose and drifted down the riverbank, knocking into one moored boat after another, setting twenty-three aflame. The fire spread to

GROUND AND BUILDINGS. **ST. LOUIS UNIVERSITY, M°** CHURCH OF S! FRANCIS XAVIER.
Fronting on Ninth Street 220 feet. On Washington Avenue and Green Street 475 feet.

St. Louis University's campus, including the original "College Church," faced Ninth Street and stretched west along Washington Avenue.

Washington University's Collegiate Hall on Washington Avenue and Seventeenth Street, as it appeared on the eve of the Civil War.

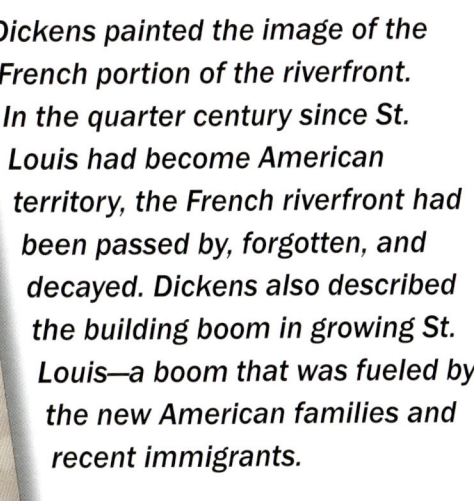

*Dickens painted the image of the French portion of the riverfront. In the quarter century since St. Louis had become American territory, the French riverfront had been passed by, forgotten, and decayed. Dickens also described the building boom in growing St. Louis—a boom that was fueled by the new American families and recent immigrants.*

"In the old French portion of the town the thoroughfares are narrow and crooked, and some of the houses are very quaint and picturesque; being built of wood, with tumble-down galleries before the windows, approachable by stairs, or rather ladders, from the street. There are queer little barbers' shops, and drinking-houses too, in this quarter; and abundance of crazy old tenements with blinking casements, such as may be seen in Flanders. Some of these ancient habitations, with high garret gable windows perking into the roofs, have a kind of French shrug about them; and, being lop-sided with age, appear to hold their heads askew besides, as if they were grimacing in astonishment at the American Improvements.

"It is hardly necessary to say that these consist of wharfs and warehouses, and new buildings in all directions; and of a great many vast plans which are still 'progressing.' Already, however, some very good houses, broad streets, and marble-fronted shops have gone so far ahead as to be in a state of completion; and the town bids fair, in a few years, to improve considerably: though it is not likely to ever vie, in point of elegance or beauty, with Cincinnati."[13]

Flames spread from steamboats and raged through downtown St. Louis on May 17 and 18, 1849, destroying 23 steamboats, and 430 buildings. The map below Leopold Gast's illustration of the fire shows the blocks of downtown St. Louis devastated by the conflagration.

Robert Campbell, one of the most successful businessmen of nineteenth-century America, lived with his family in downtown's elegant Lucas Place.

the riverfront, and through the night residents hurriedly filled wagons with their belongings and fled from their homes.

Before the flames were suppressed, fifteen blocks of downtown St. Louis were in ashes.

The destruction made a new residential area away from the river and its commerce more attractive. Lucas Grove, a patch of trees in the midst of prairie, was subdivided as a park and adjacent Lucas Place, which would soon become home to some of the most influential people in the Midwest and also home to the Robert Campbell family, one of the wealthiest in the United States.

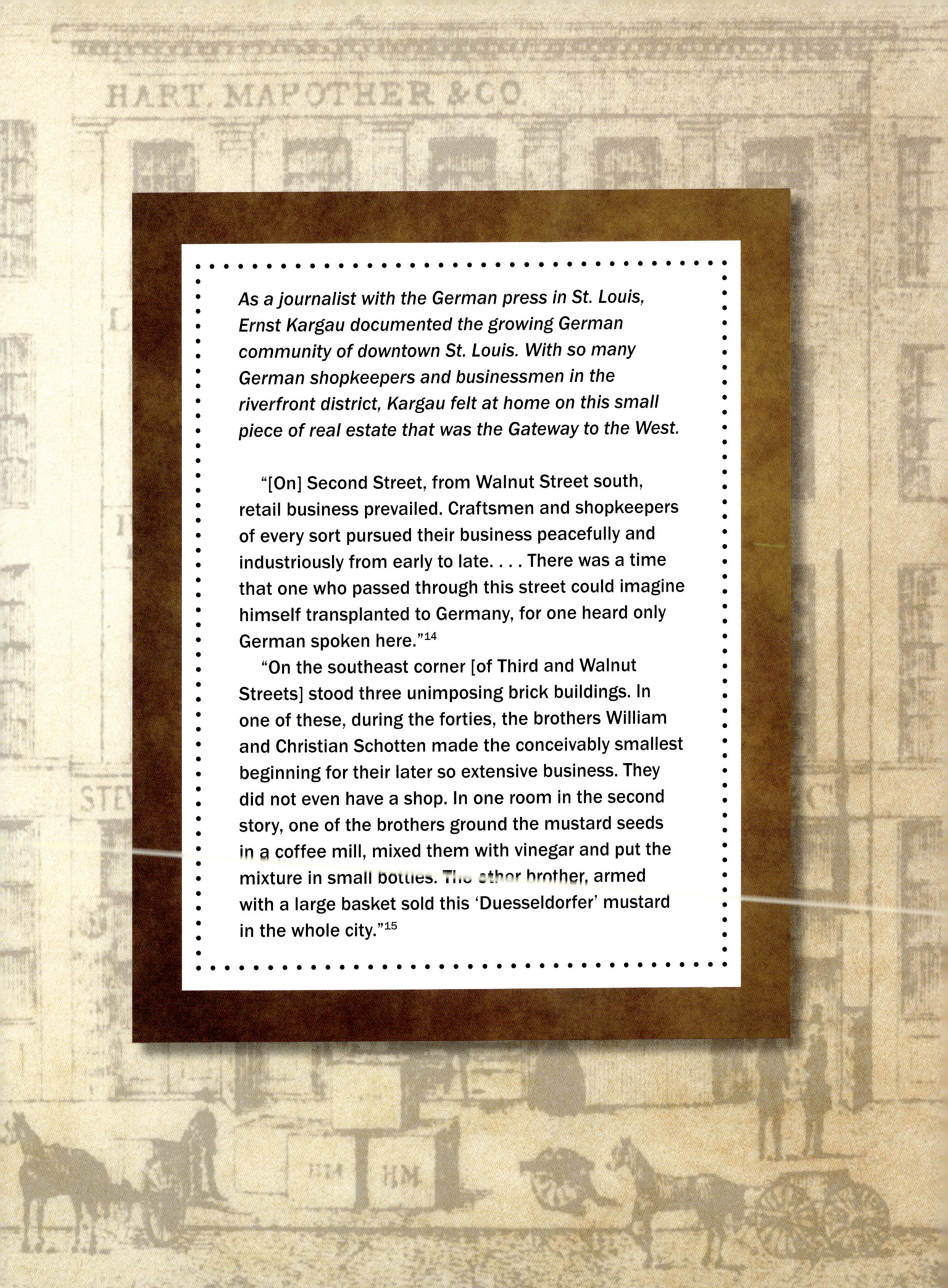

*As a journalist with the German press in St. Louis, Ernst Kargau documented the growing German community of downtown St. Louis. With so many German shopkeepers and businessmen in the riverfront district, Kargau felt at home on this small piece of real estate that was the Gateway to the West.*

"[On] Second Street, from Walnut Street south, retail business prevailed. Craftsmen and shopkeepers of every sort pursued their business peacefully and industriously from early to late. . . . There was a time that one who passed through this street could imagine himself transplanted to Germany, for one heard only German spoken here."[14]

"On the southeast corner [of Third and Walnut Streets] stood three unimposing brick buildings. In one of these, during the forties, the brothers William and Christian Schotten made the conceivably smallest beginning for their later so extensive business. They did not even have a shop. In one room in the second story, one of the brothers ground the mustard seeds in a coffee mill, mixed them with vinegar and put the mixture in small bottles. The other brother, armed with a large basket sold this 'Duesseldorfer' mustard in the whole city."[15]

VIEW ON LUCAS PLACE.

The mansions of St. Louis's elite lined Lucas Place in 1860.

The fire transformed the riverfront itself. New streets replaced the ragged ones that had made their way up the limestone terraces. Tall brick warehouses with ornamental cast-iron facades filled the grid of blocks to the sidewalk's edge. New and efficient, these warehouses powered westward expansion.

Thousands worked on the levee loading and unloading boats. Sometimes, the boats moored in double rows, forcing passengers to pass through a second boat to disembark. When a steamboat arrived, the carriages waiting at the courthouse hastened to the levee to pick up passengers. The large hotels regularly sent their own carriages to the levee to receive travelers. The levee was so covered with barrels, boxes, and bales of ware that only narrow passageways were left for the trams and wagons to get through, and even pedestrians had to zigzag their way among them.

St. Louis had a population of 160,000 when the Confederates fired on Fort Sumter in 1861. The Civil War virtually silenced the riverfront, shuttering warehouses and halting business. The river, the lifeblood of St. Louis, was shut down. Gradually, the local economy changed to make St. Louis the staging area of the western theater of the Civil War. The riverboats loaded on the St. Louis levee supplied the Union armies in the West. Hospital boats carried thousands of wounded back from Shiloh and the Siege of Vicksburg to convalesce in St. Louis.

*Author and historian Francis Parkman's trip along the Oregon Trail began in St. Louis in the spring of 1846. His account of that exploration of the American West became the best-selling book* The Oregon Trail. *The book includes this description of the bustle, business, and commerce of downtown St. Louis.*

"Last spring, 1846, was a busy season in the City of St. Louis. Not only were emigrants from every part of the country preparing for the journey to Oregon and California, but an unusual number of traders were making ready their wagons and outfits for Santa Fe. Many of the emigrants, especially of those bound for California, were persons of wealth and standing. The hotels were crowded, and the gunsmiths and saddlers were kept constantly at work in providing arms and equipments for the different parties of travelers. Almost every day steamboats were leaving the levee and passing up the Missouri, crowded with passengers on their way to the frontier."[16]

The southeast corner of Seventh and Olive Streets as it appeared in 1859. Grocers and apothecaries fill the storefronts and a firehouse (with balcony) faces Seventh Street.

RESIDENCE OF CAPTAIN GRANT AND MRS. GRANT IN AND ABOUT ST. LOUIS.

*Downtown was a neighborhood, with commercial houses and private homes. The homes were the scenes of family gatherings and celebrations. Colonel Frederick Dent, who resided at his plantation, White Haven on Gravois Road, also owned a city house at Third and Cerre Streets. It was in this home that his daughter Julia married a West Point graduate, recently returned from the war with Mexico—Ulysses S. Grant.*

"My wedding was necessarily a simple one. The season was unfavorable for a large gathering, and our temporary home in St. Louis was small. We were married about eight o'clock, and received during the evening all of our old friends in the city. . . . A table was set at the end of the back parlor upon which were served ices, fruits, and all that papa's hospitality and good taste could suggest for the occasion. My wedding cake, I was assured, was a marvel of beauty. We had music, and I think two of my gay bridesmaids took a turn around the room, saying they could not resist waltzing just a round or two. My bridesmaids were my sister Nellie Dent, Sarah Walker and my cousin Julia [Boggs]. Lieutenant Grant's groomsmen were Lieutenant Cadmus Wilcox, Bernard Pratte of St. Louis and Sid Smith. The first two surrendered to General Grant at Appomattox."[17]

Following the surrender of Lee and the Army of Virginia, commerce returned to the St. Louis riverfront. The ferry service carried trainloads of goods from the east bank of the river to the St. Louis levee, where workers carried the goods from the boats to the warehouses. From morning till evening, the Wiggins Ferry Company had eight boats in service. In 1865 between forty and fifty railroad cars a day were ferried to and from East St. Louis, Illinois, and probably between a thousand and fifteen hundred persons were transferred across the river. The number of transfer trucks amounted to five and six hundred per day, and the farm wagons, which brought the products of the soil to the market at St. Louis, numbered on average two hundred a day.

Steamboats, moored nose to the levee, pack the riverfront. Barrels, bales, and crates are piled high on the levee in 1871.

The traffic and vitality of the riverfront belied the fact that following the Civil War railroads were reshaping commerce across the nation. The very river that had given birth to St. Louis blocked the railroad tracks and was stifling the city's economic future.

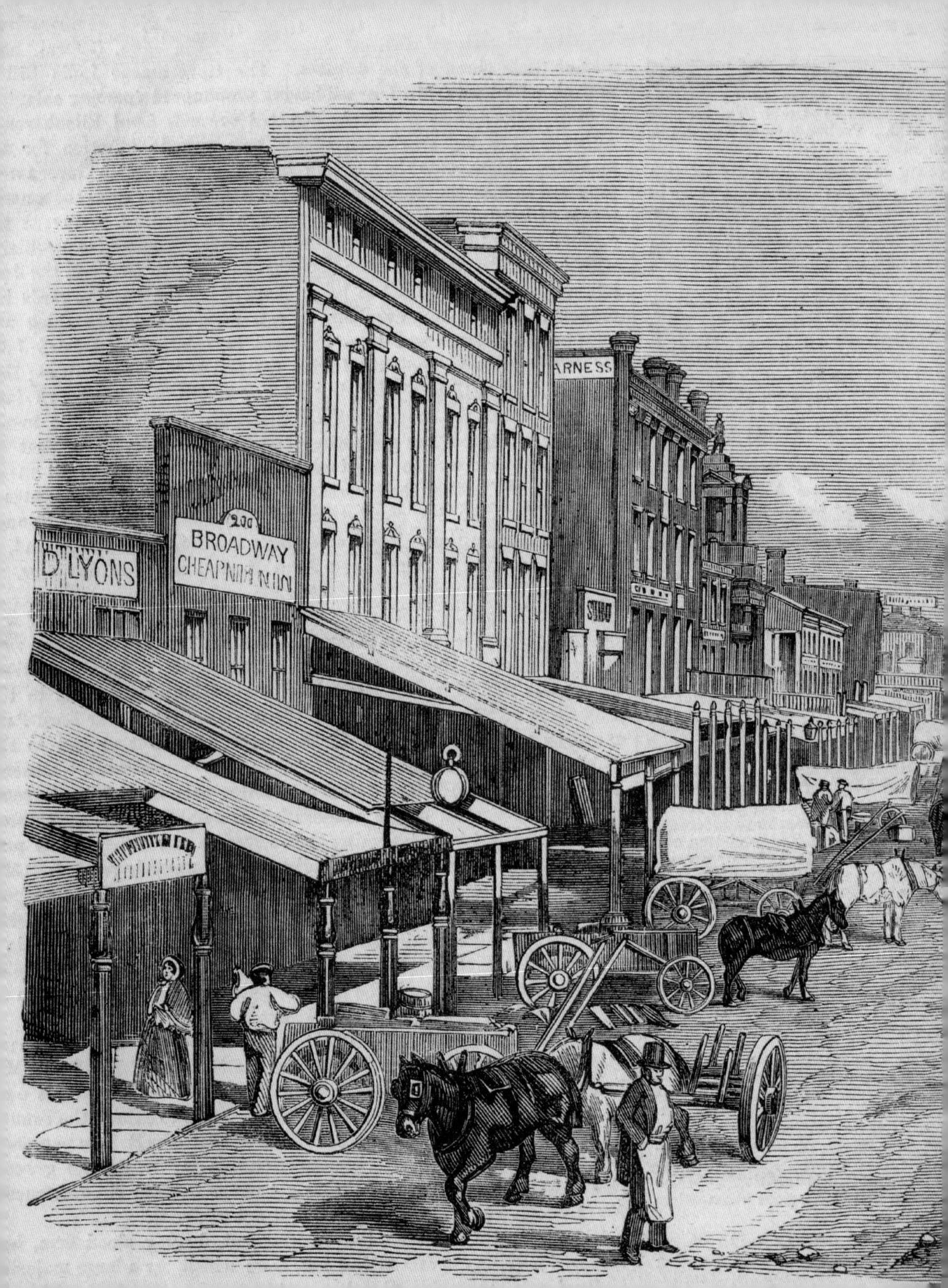

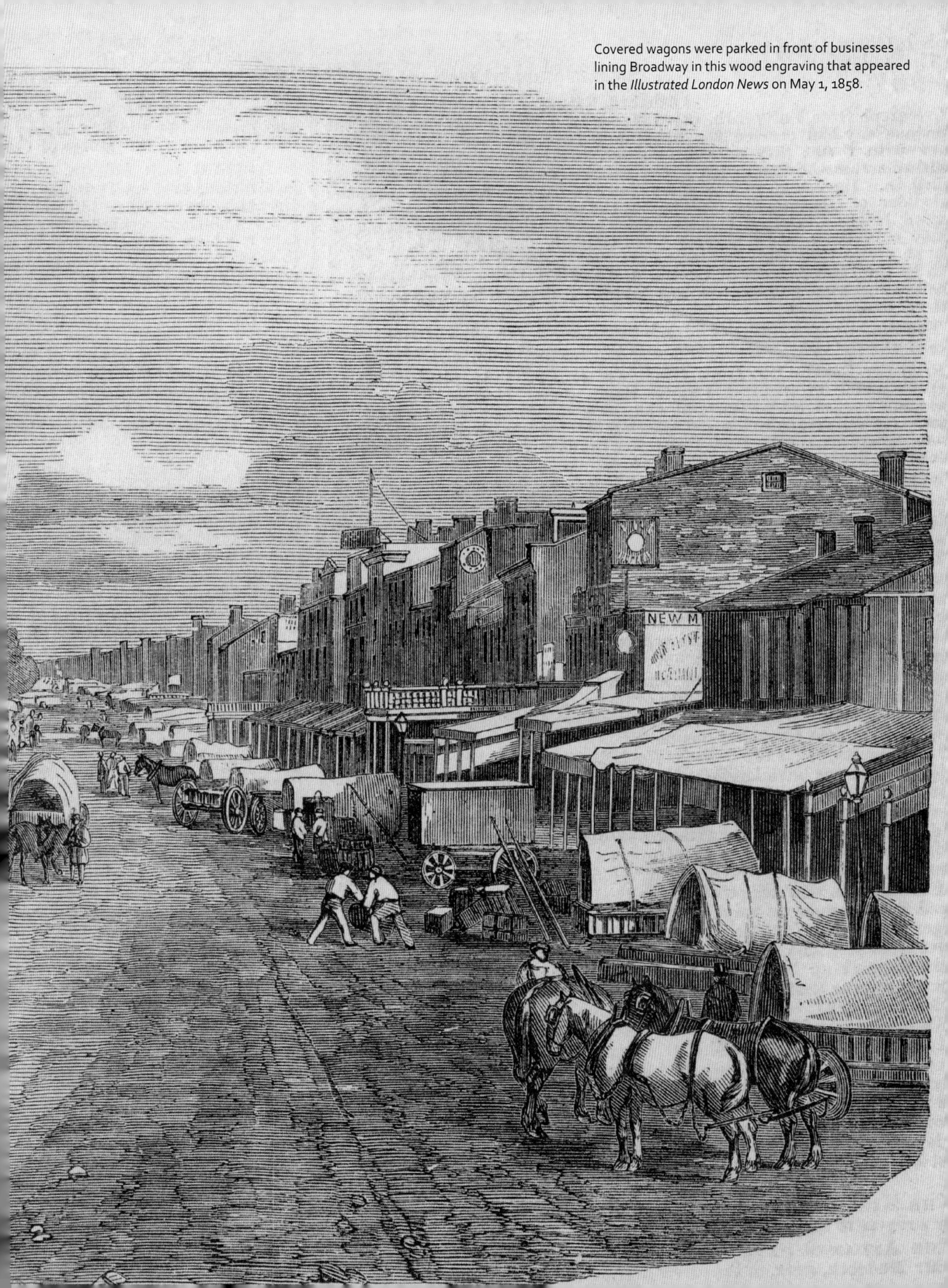

Covered wagons were parked in front of businesses lining Broadway in this wood engraving that appeared in the *Illustrated London News* on May 1, 1858.

a. Matthew Hastings watercolor from 1848 depicting Union Fire Company No. 2 and Franklin Fire Company No. 8 on parade at Fourth and Olive.

b. Buggies lined up in front of the Old Courthouse, circa 1870.

c. St. Louis was home to forty breweries in 1860, including Fritz, Wainwright & Co., located on Tenth Street at Gratiot Street.

d. Verandah Row on Washington Avenue in 1857.

e. Photograph of the busy St. Louis levee.

f. Lithograph of the levee with a French house in the background.

g. Eads Bridge under construction.

h. Mercantile Library.

i. Tony Faust's Oyster Bar.

j. Looking west on Olive Street from Fourth Street in 1848.

Mansions and townhouses are in the foreground and church steeples, the onion domes of the high school, and the dome of the Old Courthouse punctuate the skyline in this view of St. Louis looking toward the riverfront from Lucas Place.

## Chapter 3
# 1874–1916

*The* Post-Dispatch *reported both the idyllic lifestyle of Lucas Place and that the booming growth of downtown threatened its future.*

"At Fourteenth Street begins one of the beauty spots of St. Louis, commonly known as Lucas Place. For full three blocks not a shanty rears its head. All the houses are large and handsome, and the shade trees the best the city can show. The street is paved with large blocks of limestone, and is, consequently, very clean. It is an intensely quiet spot, and if children live there they are kept within doors, and are never allowed to make mud pies in the gutter. Within its limits are the First and Second Presbyterian churches. Lucas Place is yet quite exclusive, but it cannot always remain so. The city is growing towards it, and inside of twenty years it will be abandoned to keepers of first-class hash houses."[18]

Eads Bridge, the engineering marvel completed in 1874, ushered in a magnificent era for downtown St. Louis. During this era, St. Louisans filled their downtown with great architectural landmarks—the Federal Court and Custom House reflecting the Palace of Versailles, a revolutionary skyscraper, a railroad station that was modeled after the walled medieval city of Carcassonne, and a city hall inspired by that of Paris. Every new building—whether a warehouse on Washington Avenue or a bank building on Fourth Street—was a civic ornament.

The completed engineering marvel, the Eads Bridge, as it appeared in Compton and Dry's *Pictorial St. Louis*.

Understanding that St. Louis's economy required the bridging of the mighty Mississippi, self-taught engineer James B. Eads inspired and led the effort to form a bridge company in 1866. At a time when one in every four bridges collapsed, St. Louisans built the

*The music of the streets was reported by local journalists J. A. Dacus and James W. Buel when they wrote about the street vendors of St. Louis.*

"The trade in tropical fruits and in nuts is largely in the hands of Italians, who are altogether the most successful vendors of such things on the street. Some of them perambulate the streets, while others are fixed at corner-stalls. Some of them select a favorite corner and stop their perambulator in the gutter, while they continually cry out the quality and price of the fruits, nuts, etc., which they offer for sale to the passing throngs. Some of these street cries are quite musical, and, uttered by the soft-voiced sons of Italy, the effect produced is not unpleasing. 'Pea nu-tee! Frez ro-asted pee nut-tee! On-ee five cent a quart!' The cadences employed in these efforts at commercial oratory are very pleasing and not unfrequently effective."[19]

biggest bridge ever constructed and the first one built of alloy steel. Its three great arched spans rested on four stone piers. The center span measured 520 feet and was flanked by spans measuring 502 feet. Its dedication on July 4, 1874, was a spectacle that attracted national attention.

The Eads Bridge, with its mighty stone piers and arcs of steel, conquered the Mississippi.

With railroads fueling the national economy, this railroad bridge secured the city's role as an economic powerhouse. It also reshaped the growth of downtown St. Louis.

The bridge crossed high above the levee, carrying wagon and train traffic over the warehouses lining the riverfront. At Fourth Street, once the western edge of the village of St. Louis, the bridge directed wagon traffic directly onto Washington Avenue. That spurred massive development along that street for decades. The rail deck sent train traffic into a tunnel that emerged at Eighth Street and Clark Avenue. The rail traffic spurred the development of the massive Cupples warehouses along Clark Avenue west to Eleventh Street. Though the levee still buzzed after the opening of Eads Bridge, it was never again the heart of commerce.

**BRIDGE CELEBRATION.**

*Admit ONE to the Bridge,*

During the Passage of the Procession Only.

**GEORGE BAIN.**
*Chairman Bridge Committee.*

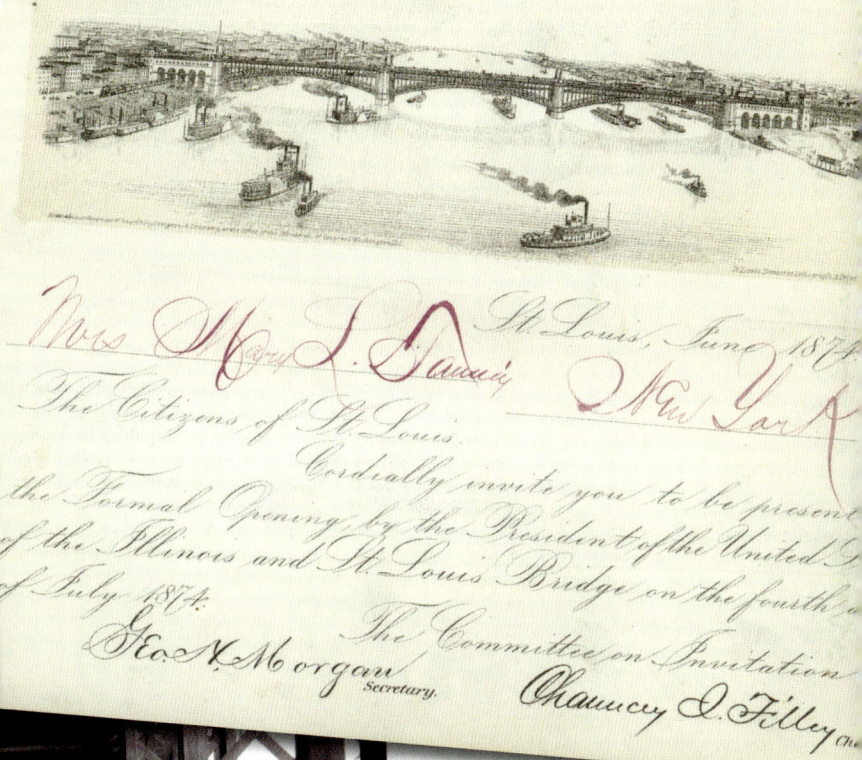

Mrs. Mary L. Davis, St. Louis, June 1874, New York

The Citizens of St. Louis Cordially invite you to be present at the Formal Opening, by the President of the United States, of the Illinois and St. Louis Bridge on the fourth of July 1874.

Geo. H. Morgan, Secretary
Chauncey I. Filley, Chairman
The Committee on Invitation

the bustling levee, St. Louis, where the products of the Mississippi ... are distributed.

No. 2325    Not Transferable.

N. B:—It is expected you will endorse your name on the back of this Ticket before presentation.

**ADMIT THE BEARER TO SPECIAL TRAIN,**
Leaving the Vandalia Depot, East Saint Louis, July 4th, 1874, at Nine o'clock A. M., sharp.

George Bain, Chairman.

A streetscape lined with massive Cupples warehouses. At one time Cupples Station consisted of eighteen warehouses, closely spaced, and designed for rapid freight handling. They were built near the mouth of the rail tunnel leading from Eads Bridge.

While Washington Avenue bustled with growing commerce from the bridge traffic, nearby Lucas Place, stretching from Fourteenth to Eighteenth Streets, maintained a dignified and elegant lifestyle. Residents set aside Wednesdays for visiting on Lucas Place. From late November through Ash Wednesday, the lady of the house served fine liquors, cake, and tea, while coal fires warmed the gracious parlors. Lawn tennis was a popular summer entertainment. In 1875, author Edward King described Lucas Place as "the Fifth Avenue of St. Louis, and is very rich in costly homes surrounded by noble gardens."[20]

The massive new Exposition Hall was opened at Thirteenth and Olive Streets in 1884. The three-story brick, terra-cotta, and stone hall was described as "peculiarly elegant." Its music hall could seat four thousand people and had standing room for another two thousand. Saddlers, cattlemen in cowboy hats, physicians, and the Saengerbund (German singing society) held their national conventions in the hall. The latest innovations in technology were discussed at photography conventions and at the meeting of the National Electric Light Association. In 1887 Civil War veterans held the Grand Army of the Republic reunion there. And in 1888, the Democratic Party chose Grover Cleveland as their candidate for president of the United States in the Exposition Hall.

The St. Louis Exposition Hall was built on the eastern half of Missouri Park, on Olive Street at Thirteenth, in 1884.

A souvenir with portraits of President and Mrs. Cleveland from the 1888 National Democratic Convention held at the St. Louis Exposition Hall.

The view from the gallery at the hall bedecked with bunting and flags for the Democratic Convention, as it appeared in *Harper's Weekly*, June 16, 1888.

*In her grand home on Lucas Place (1508 Locust Street), Virginia Campbell served champagne punch to her dinner guests, which included General William Tecumseh Sherman and President Ulysses S. Grant.*

<u>Virginia Campbell's Roman Punch</u>
1 cup cold water
1 cup white sugar
4 large lemons
1 large orange
3 egg whites
6 ounces champagne or sparkling wine

1. Place water in a heavy saucepan over a low heat; sprinkle in sugar and swirl until it dissolves. Bring to a boil for five minutes.
2. Grate zest of lemons and oranges and add to sugar water mixture. Squeeze juice from lemons and orange, and add to sugar mixture. Let stand until cool. (There should be at least ½ cup of lemon juice and ⅓ cup of orange juice.)
3. Beat egg whites with a whisk until foamy but not to the soft peak stage. Add to sugar juice mixture.
4. Strain mixture into a non-aluminum container, add champagne, cover, and freeze. When mixture begins to freeze, stir occasionally until completely frozen.
5. Serve scooped into small glass bowls or saucer champagne glasses.

Makes 4 servings.

Sadly, the hall was built on one of the few large available sites in downtown, the south half of lovely Missouri Park (later known as Lucas Park). The traffic to its concert and convention halls began eroding the nearby residential areas, especially Lucas Place.

Great office buildings replaced the old houses along Fourth, Broadway, Sixth, and Seventh Streets. The federal government pulled the epicenter of business farther west with the construction of the then new Federal Court and Custom House (the Old Post Office). The four-story courthouse, which required twelve years to build, covered the block framed by Eighth, Olive, Ninth, and Locust Streets. When it was completed in 1884, with columns on all four sides and a mansard roof topped by a glowing white sculpture, its style and scale dominated its immediate surroundings.

St. Louisans lined the riverbank to greet President Theodore Roosevelt, who arrived by the steamer *Mississippi* on October 27, 1907.

At the turn of the century, electric streetcars along with horse-drawn wagons fueled business on Washington Avenue near Fifth Street, the hub of the dry goods and department stores.

During the 1890s, monumental warehouse and office buildings replaced the smaller commercial buildings on Washington Avenue and filled the blocks left vacant when St. Louis University moved its campus west to Grand Avenue. Huge piers of rusticated stone dominated the street level of the buildings, and heavy cornices with terra-cotta trim topped the buildings. Warehouses for the tobacco

Horse-drawn street railway line on Fourth Street. Buggies lined the curb in front of the Old Courthouse.

industry, shoe industry, and dry goods businesses soon dominated the street. Mules and horses pulled wagons loaded with dry goods across the streetcar tracks, which carried warehouse laborers to their jobs on Washington Avenue.

At the same time, St. Louisans were building a revolutionary masterpiece of American architecture—the Wainwright Building at Seventh and Chestnut Streets. With the Wainwright Building, Chicago architect Louis Sullivan spiritually created the skyscraper. Thanks to steel frame construction coupled with elevators, American builders had been able to build higher and higher, but they were just adding floors. Their tall buildings with repetitive designs looked like wedding cakes, while Sullivan's new ten-story building on Seventh Street celebrated its height.

Architect Louis Sullivan captured the potential of skyscraper design with his design for the Wainwright Building. With this skyscraper on Seventh Street, he created a new architectural idiom that was thoroughly American.

*Only a few blocks from Louis Sullivan's Wainwright Building and Union Trust Building was the center of St. Louis's small Chinese community. The seeds of the colony, known as Hop Alley, dated to the Chinese immigrant workers who helped build the transcontinental railroad. Hop Alley was mysterious, exotic, and closed, perhaps responding to roundups of Chinese illegals. The* Post-Dispatch *described the community in an article on the challenges Chinatown posed to census takers in 1910.*

"Census taking in Hop Alley—a Hop Alley that is but a mere shadow of the lively, pulsating community it was a few years ago, is a thankless and unprofitable job at best. So thinks Census Enumerator Edward L Tobin . . . who, after five hours of painstaking work, with an interpreter, managed to record 142 Chinese residents.

"Low, dark unventilated rooms form the Chinese haven and as aid to the gloom, if there be a window to an apartment, it is never washed. Caked dust invariably spreads itself over Chinese window panes, serving as a barrier to the sun's rays. . . .

Colorful and mysterious, St. Louis's small Chinatown at Market and Eighth Streets was known as Hop Alley. It was wedged between Skid Row and Prizefighters' Row.

"While there were, perhaps, one hundred and fifty Chinese about Hop Alley, which extends from Seventh to Ninth street, between Market and Walnut streets, that figure does not represent the population there. In most of the houses, which were formerly opium dens, testified to by the bunks and "dope" layouts therein, a single Chinese appeared. . . .

"Most of [the Chinese] in St. Louis maintain quarters in and about Hop Alley, but work about the city in laundries. On Sunday afternoons it is customary for many to visit the alley to smoke, play fantan and indulge in the offerings of the Chinese restaurants, which abound in the vicinity."[21]

A rooftop garden in downtown St. Louis in 1894.

Architect Louis Sullivan used snowflake designs in the ornamental terra-cotta panels on his third masterpiece in downtown St. Louis, the St. Nicholas Hotel.

Round windows peek through the lavish terra-cotta covering the top floor cornice of the Wainwright Building.

When the Wainwright was ready for occupancy in the fall of 1892, it boasted 250 offices and towered over much of downtown. More than its scale, the building's magic came from the combination of lavish ornament and vertical lines that pointed to the sky.

Near this pioneer of the modern skyscraper, two more remarkable skyscrapers designed by Sullivan soon punctuated the St. Louis skyline. The St. Nicholas Hotel and the Union Trust Building were both completed in 1893.

Perhaps in respect of Sullivan's precedent-shattering designs in St. Louis, the American Institute of Architects held their national convention at the St. Nicholas Hotel in 1895. (The building was razed in 1973.) The architects attending the convention arrived at St. Louis's new Union Station, opened only the year before. While Sullivan's skyscrapers and downtown's other great skyscrapers were palaces of commerce and home to business elite, Union Station served the entire community. The station's opening was a community festivity.

At the grand opening of Union Station on September 1, 1894, St. Louisans relished the experience of the extravagant Grand Hall with its stained glass, ornamental iron, molded plaster work, mosaic tiles, faience block walls, stenciling, and gold leafing.

Portrait of German St. Louisan Theodore Link, the architect of Union Station.

On September 1, 1894, the electric streetcar lines unloaded thousands of people near the Eighteenth Street and Market Street entrance to the new Union Station, the largest railroad station in the world. Crowds packed the walks and streets waiting for the opening of the two-block-wide station that resembled a French medieval castle. Private carriages clattered over the pavements from the West End and unloaded their fashionable occupants under the porte cochere at the main entrance.

The station, designed by German St. Louisan Theodore Link, opened at 7:30 p.m. Crowds pushed their way up the long terraces and through the doors to be dazzled. In the Grand Hall, a vaulted ceiling rose over the immense space. With great ribs

The construction of the huge Union Station required 3,000,000 pounds of steel, 6,000,000 nails, and 1,000,000 square feet of plaster. Its clock tower stands 230 feet tall.

of gold, an arcaded gallery, lunette windows, and clusters of columns capped with gold, the Grand Hall left people breathless. The Terminal Railroad Association estimated that between 45,000 and 50,000 visited Union Station on opening night.

With a population of 450,000 residents, the fourth-largest city in the nation was outgrowing its old city hall at Eleventh and Market Streets. Downtown's booming growth left little space available for a monumental civic building. Facing the same dilemma city leaders had faced with building the Exposition Hall, they chose the same solution of using parkland. In 1891 the cornerstone was laid for the new city hall on the site of Washington Square at Twelfth and Market Streets.

Remarkably, the construction was funded out of the annual city budget over

Animals were still herded through the city streets at the turn of the century as shown in this photo of hogs being herded at Market and Thirteenth Streets.

the next fourteen years. The spectacular new St. Louis City Hall, modeled after the city hall of Paris, was dedicated on November 5, 1904.

By 1909, Broadway was the chief shopping thoroughfare, banks were concentrated on Fourth Street, retail trade centered on Olive Street, printing offices were located on Third Street, commission houses were on First and Second Streets along the river, and retail and wholesale trade revolved around Washington Avenue.

The *Realty Record and Builder* described the construction boom on Washington Avenue in 1911. "The expansion of the great wholesale houses of Washington Avenue during the past four years has made this thoroughfare the center of St. Louis' greatest building activity. The growth of this thoroughfare has been marvelous. There have been several causes for this, chief among which was the legitimate expansion of all of the wholesale dry goods and

The grand staircase of Italian marble is the focal point of city hall's elegant, four-story rotunda that is encircled by balustraded balconies.

The neoclassical-style chambers of the Board of Aldermen are highlighted by medallion portraits of prominent St. Louisans and lunettes filled with scenes of St. Louis's industry, education, and founding.

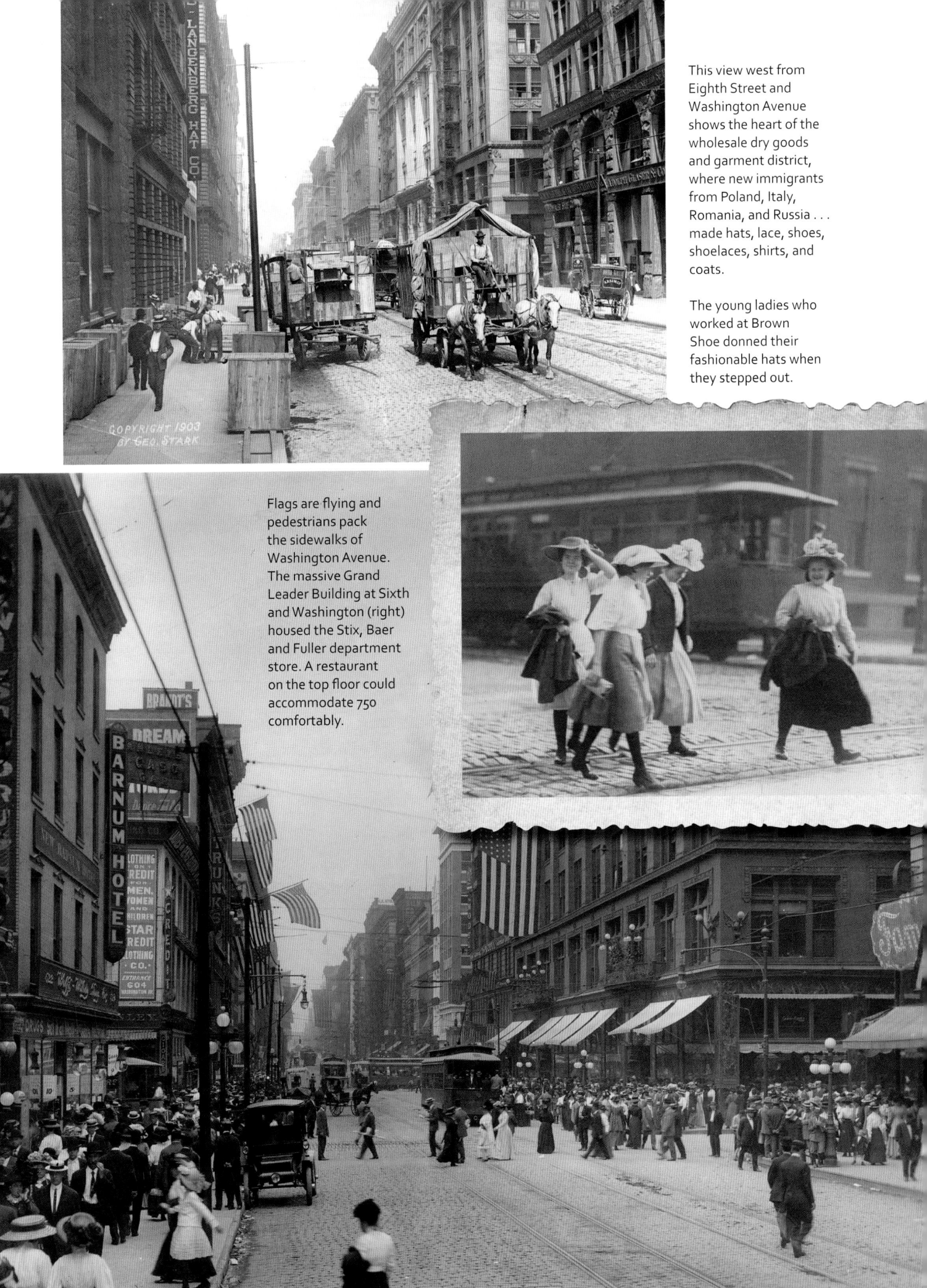

This view west from Eighth Street and Washington Avenue shows the heart of the wholesale dry goods and garment district, where new immigrants from Poland, Italy, Romania, and Russia . . . made hats, lace, shoes, shoelaces, shirts, and coats.

The young ladies who worked at Brown Shoe donned their fashionable hats when they stepped out.

Flags are flying and pedestrians pack the sidewalks of Washington Avenue. The massive Grand Leader Building at Sixth and Washington (right) housed the Stix, Baer and Fuller department store. A restaurant on the top floor could accommodate 750 comfortably.

Even in an era of great civic buildings, the St. Louis Public Library was a stunning monument to civic pride and enlightenment. Completed in 1912, the exterior walls of Maine granite bear the trademarks of thirty-six early printers, from Johann Gutenberg to Benjamin Franklin.

Translucent cathedral glass windows and the gold highlighted ceiling in the library's Delivery Hall accent the pink in Tennessee marble sheathing the walls. The ornate, molded plaster ceiling was inspired by Italian Renaissance designs.

shoe houses of the city, making larger buildings a necessity."[22]

Each year shopkeepers from small towns throughout the Midwest and West came to Washington Avenue to stock their stores. They traveled by train, stayed at downtown hotels, and examined the displays in the huge dry goods warehouses on Washington Avenue. They ordered dresses, shoes, brooms, scrub boards, linens, cast-iron stoves, cookware, and hardware that they then sold to townspeople, settlers, and ranchers.

Only a city block south of the thriving garment district, the library system opened its classic Central Library in 1912. With Renaissance-era libraries of Europe as inspiration for its design elements, the library was downtown's temple of learning.

In 1908, crowds gathered at Twelfth Street and Delmar for a campaign visit by presidential contender William Howard Taft.

While German bricklayers, Irish hod carriers, and Bohemian and Croatian stonemasons were filling downtown with architectural gems meant for the ages, downtown St. Louis was not a pristine place. Ethnic communities rooted in the Deep South and central Europe, often crowded into tenements, brought downtown their raw energy.

The largest of the tenements, the four-story Ashley tenement, covered half a block at the northeast corner of downtown at Broadway and Biddle Street. The old tenement, with 210 rooms, had been a port of entry for generations of Irish immigrants. By the turn of the century, it almost exclusively housed emigrants from Poland. The *Post-Dispatch* reported that in 1902, "513 people huddled together in this big, barnlike structure." While some rooms were vacant, other single-room units housed up to twelve immigrants. The *Post-Dispatch* article editorialized, "Owing to the excitable nature of the Poles, it has always been necessary to

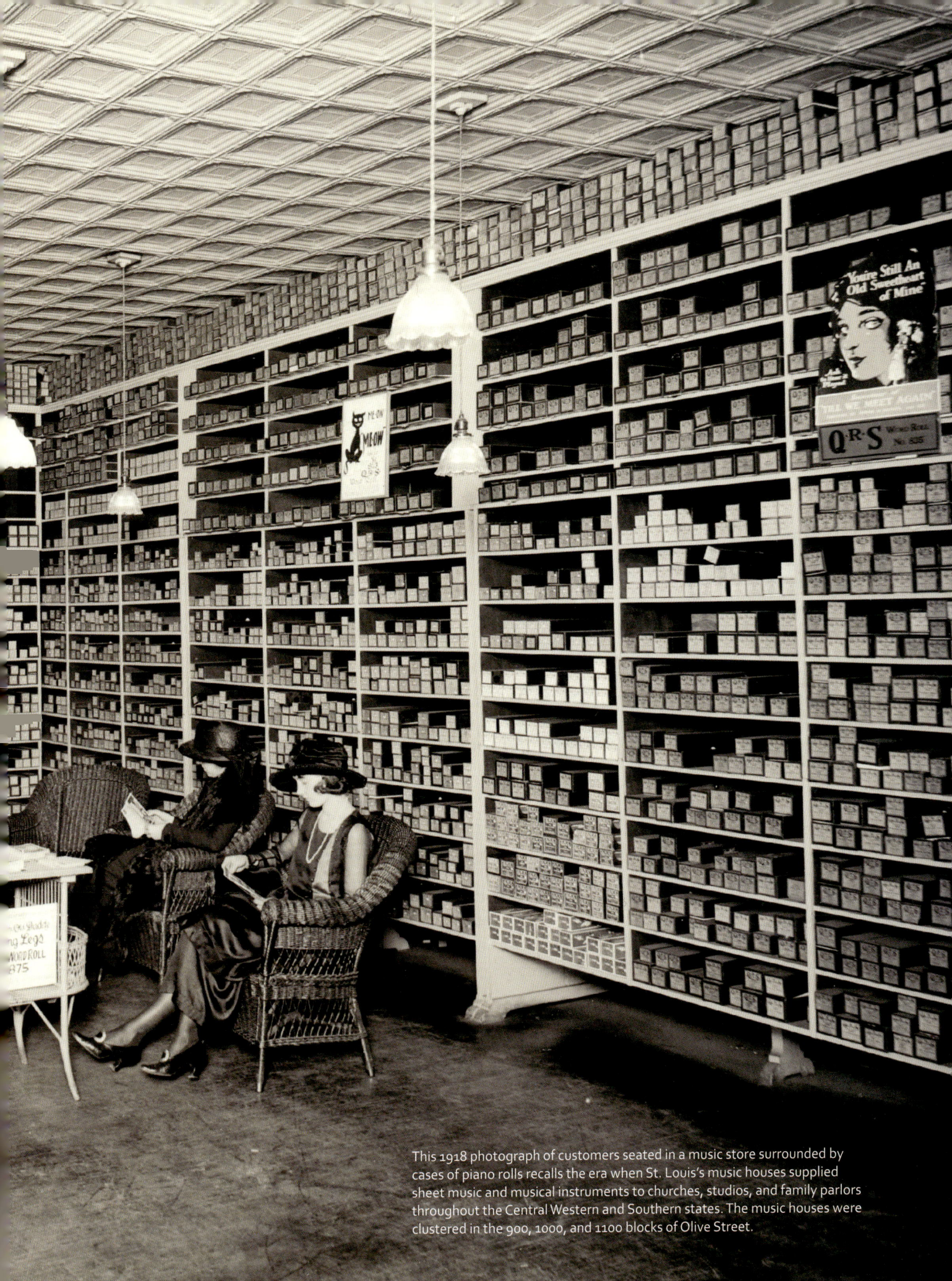

This 1918 photograph of customers seated in a music store surrounded by cases of piano rolls recalls the era when St. Louis's music houses supplied sheet music and musical instruments to churches, studios, and family parlors throughout the Central Western and Southern states. The music houses were clustered in the 900, 1000, and 1100 blocks of Olive Street.

maintain a policeman at the Ashley tenement" and noted the regular Saturday night dances at the building that lasted well into the night.[23] The officers assigned to the building were Michael Manikowski, who was fluent in the Polish, Bohemian, and Russian languages, and Stanislaus Wardenski, who was fluent in the Polish, Bohemian, Russian, Hungarian, and Slavic tongues.

Flophouses, liveries, factories, and offices were replacing the townhouses, trees, and ornamental iron fences of the western area of downtown around St. John the Apostle and Centenary Methodist Churches. While the buildings were dilapidated and neglected, a new rhythmic music poured out of the windows of the nearby saloons and honky-tonks. The "Bards of Chestnut Street"[24] created songs out of local events. For a tip or a drink, these piano players and singers performed their ballad. One of those ballads, "Frankie and Johnnie," caught the public's fancy. The King of the Piano, Tom Turpin, opened the Rosebud Cafe at 2220 Market Street in 1900. His composition, "Harlem Rag" published in 1897, is considered the first published rag by an African American. His saloon on Market Street soon became a gathering place and catalyst for African American pianists creating ragtime music, which later fathered jazz.

Despite the outstanding architecture of downtown, the vibrant commerce, and energy of its residents, much of the remaining housing was overcrowded with inadequate plumbing. Coal pollution from both furnaces and industry blackened the air. The streets department was experimenting with pavement despite the choking streetcar and wagon traffic. The congregation of Centenary Methodist Church decided to keep their church at its location at Pine and Sixteenth Streets. Its members were coming from all sections of the city to the beautiful stone church despite nearby honky-tonks and houses of ill repute.

Beginning in 1907, civic leadership developed a series of plans and efforts to sweep away some of the decayed areas. After using park space for civic buildings in the late nineteenth century, they proposed uniting the new civic buildings—city hall, Union Station, and the Central Library—with new parks and plazas. The rows of trees and greenery would filter the air, provide needed outdoor space for residents and workers, and create an appropriate setting for great civic buildings. These early plans were the seed of a ribbon of parks and public uses that would eventually connect the riverfront with Union Station.

The provocative terra-cotta cornice of the Bee Hat Building, built in 1899 at 1025 Washington Avenue, features bosomy females.

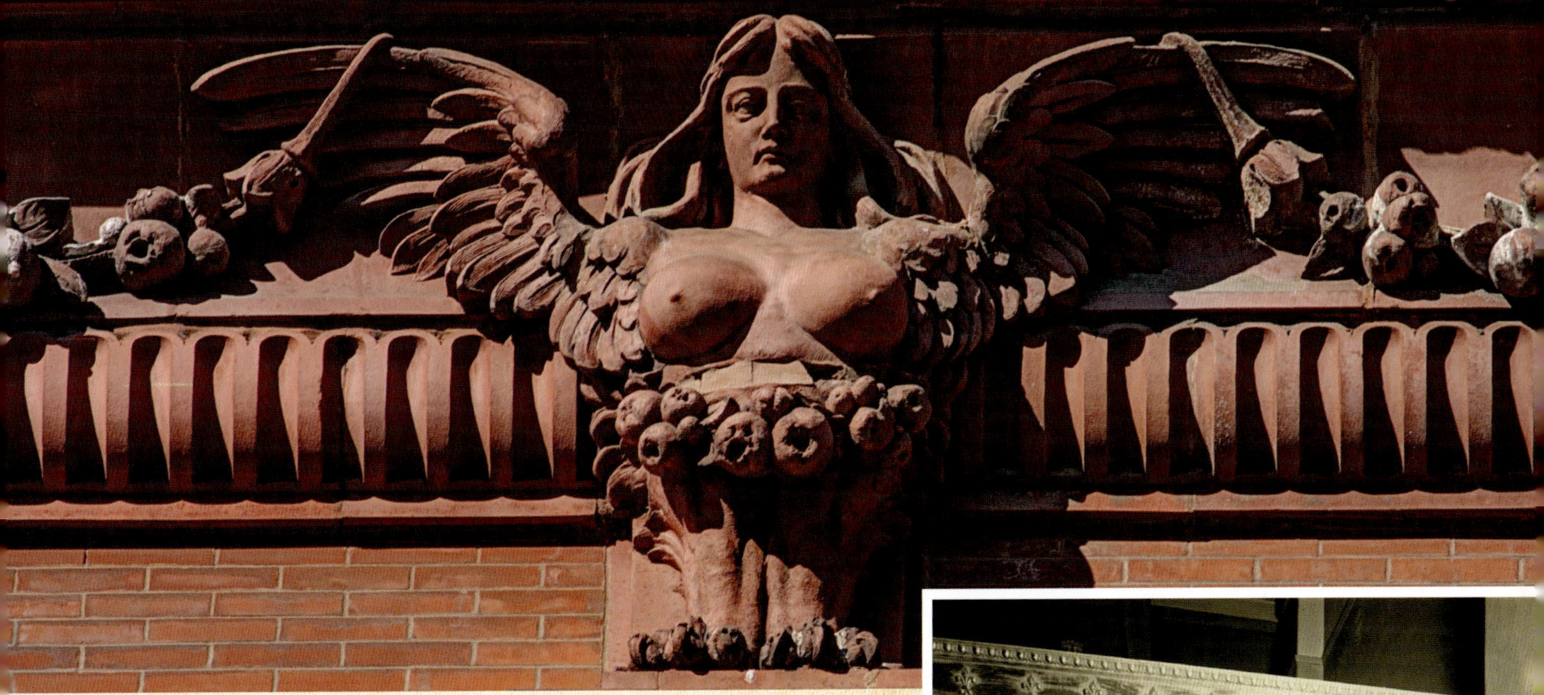

The new generation of downtown buildings dwarfed the then forgotten buildings of the riverfront, the early commercial structures, and the remaining townhouses still scattered around the fringes of downtown. These extraordinary new buildings housed enormous stores, hotels, banks, and offices; served as warehouses; and were home to civic business. This incarnation of downtown St. Louis boasted a bountiful collection of great architecture that would be a gift to future generations.

The teller at the payment window at the Southwestern Bell Building.

The Missouri Athletic Club opened its doors on September 13, 1903, with the goal of becoming "the premier athletic, social and dining club for business, professional and civic leaders and their families in the St. Louis area." Soon the spectacular new club was hosting dignitaries from around the world who were visiting St. Louis for the Olympics and World's Fair. Athletes from the MAC competed in boxing, wrestling, water polo, swimming, and track at the Olympic Games.

A tragic fire destroyed the original clubhouse in March 1914. Within weeks, members were planning a new, grander clubhouse to be built on the same site. Architect William B. Ittner, who was gaining a national reputation for his innovative designs for school buildings, designed a ten-story building that would dominate its corner at Washington and Fourth Street. A massive, bracketed cornice topped the club, which featured stone arches facing the street and floors of patterned brickwork.

Five thousand people attended the gala opening of the downtown clubhouse on March 1, 1916.

Over the following decades, club athletes won Olympic medals and national AAU events. Early MAC athletes like Joseph Forshaw, Harry Kiener, and Culver Halstedt became known far beyond the boundaries of St. Louis.

In 2000, the MAC was awarded "Platinum Club" status for the first time. This designation takes into consideration the quality of membership, tradition and heritage, facilities, amenities, club management, and staff. With this award, the MAC has distinguished itself as among the top 3 percent of private clubs in the country every year since.

The stag smoker held on November 23, 1937, included a steak dinner with a German band providing the early entertainment and a mixed set of boxing and wrestling matches for later in the evening. More than seven hundred packed the ballroom for the event.

Curiosity seekers gather at the wreck of a lumber company wagon at Twelfth and Pine Streets.

a. Girls in flamboyant hats in the warehouse district.
b. Opening of Famous in 1892.
c. Alley traffic in the warehouse district.
d. Experiments with street paving.
e. National Suffrage Day, 1914.
f. Tony Faust's Cafe and Oyster Bar.

The warehouses lining the levee that had powered river commerce in the mid-nineteenth century stood grimy and underutilized in the early twentieth century. The massive new towers of commerce lined Fourth, Broadway, Sixth, and Seventh Streets.

## Chapter 4

# 1917-1945

St. Louis poet Sarah Teasdale wrote "Sunset: St. Louis" in 1920. In the poem, she described the St. Louis riverfront and skyline and even the haze created by coal smoke.

Sunset: St. Louis

Hushed in the smoky haze of summer sunset,
When I came home again from far-off places,
How many times I saw my western city.
Dream by her river.

Then for an hour the water wore a mantle
Of tawny gold and mauve and misted turquoise
Under the tall and darkened arches bearing
Gray, high-flung bridges.

Against the sunset, water-towers and steeples
Flickered with fire up the slope to westward,
And old warehouses poured their purple shadows
Across the levee.

High over them the black train swept with thunder,
Cleaving the city, leaving far beneath it
Wharf-boats moored beside the old side-wheelers
Resting in twilight.[25]

When the nation entered World War I in 1917, wagons, trucks, and early automobiles choked the narrow streets between the warehouses and office buildings of downtown St. Louis. Immigrants and their adult children powered downtown businesses. Conversations on the streetcars converging at the warehouses on Washington Avenue were in the Italian, Yiddish, Polish, and Russian tongues. Greeks operated candy shops. German, Italian, and Irish parish churches were at the northern edge of downtown, and Lebanese and Slavic communities framed the southern edge.

The World War marked a change in how St. Louisans viewed themselves. They still spoke German or Czech at home or at the bakery shop or tavern, but after so many had donned the uniform of the American doughboy, the young generation identified more with America than their ancestral homeland.

In a burst of civic enthusiasm, these citizens passed a huge bond issue in 1923 that included $6 million to create a plaza and construct a downtown memorial dedicated to the St. Louisans who had lost their lives in World War I. The

A fruit and produce peddler pulls his wagon onto Broadway near Cerre Street at the southern edge of downtown, where mid-nineteenth-century buildings still framed the streets.

memorial, however, was part of a major change in the building of downtown. With this bond issue, streets were widened to make room for cars. Instead of subtracting parking space, the bond issue funded new parkland and plazas. St. Louisans adopted the new art deco style with its sweeping curves and geometric shapes to fashion new skyscrapers and civic buildings.

The booming twenties saw the construction of Southwestern Bell's 369-foot 1010 Pine building and the Missouri Pacific (MoPac) Building at Thirteenth and Olive Streets with its shiny white terra-cotta. These new skyscrapers looked nothing like the generation of skyscrapers inspired by Louis Sullivan with the Wainwright Building. Instead of projecting cornices, stepped rooflines topped these skyscrapers and cut designs into the skyline. The walls of these new downtown skyscrapers were shades of light gray and tan rather than the rich colors of their predecessors. Their terra-cotta ornament formed the streamlined and stylized designs of the art deco movement.

Washington Avenue's industry continued to grow,

The dramatic, geometric, and streamlined designs of the art deco movement inspired the bold architecture of Soldiers' Memorial, built to honor the men who had served and died in the Great War.

New York–style setbacks gave the massive Missouri Pacific Building, built in 1928, a stepped roofline.

Banjo, brass, and woodwind musicians on the steps of city hall accompany flappers with bobbed hair and their partners in a Charleston dance contest held on November 13, 1925.

Immigrants found jobs as seamstresses in workshops like the Consolidated Garment Company sewing workshop pictured in 1919. It was located at 1224 Washington Avenue.

employing thousands of people. Sam and Rose Pollock, owners of the Pollock Clothing Company, developed the Fashion Square Building at 1307 Washington Avenue. Opened in 1926, the eleven-story building housed numerous clothing buyers and manufacturers, including their own company. They hired Jewish immigrants from eastern Europe who worked as cutters or at sewing machines, and as pressers who ironed the garments. They made men's suits and topcoats. Like Pollock, they spoke Yiddish. As many as nine hundred people worked in the Gothic Revival building that boasted eighteen thousand square feet of floor space.

Built in 1926, the impressive Paul Brown Building originally offered 250,000 square feet of office space. The building completed the then modern office district surrounding the Federal Court and Custom House, later called the Old Post Office.

The area framing the Federal Building (Old Post Office) at Eighth and Olive Streets was a hub of activity with offices and department stores. The Federal Building had dominated its surroundings when it was completed in 1884. By 1926, with the completion of the adjacent Paul Brown Building, the old Federal Building was like a jewel at the center of a lavish setting of great buildings that featured Roman-arched doorways, Tudor-arched windows, wildly ornate red terra-cotta, ornate cast-iron storefronts, and cream-colored sculptures.

"It was an exciting time to be in St. Louis," lifelong South St. Louisan Billie Baudissin said of the late 1920s. Not only was there a building boom, the city erupted into a party that lasted days when the baseball Cardinals, formerly the laugh of the National League, won their first pennant and World Series in

The Washington/Delmar double-decker bus served downtown along with the streetcars during the Roaring Twenties. The women on the bus and sidewalks are wearing fashionable cloche hats and many of the men have donned summer straw hats.

the fall of 1926. Then Charles Lindbergh's epic transatlantic flight in his St. Louis–financed *Spirit of St. Louis* single-engine plane was celebrated across Europe. When Lindbergh returned to St. Louis, five thousand policemen were needed to line his victory parade through the half million cheering St. Louisans who lined his route through downtown's narrow streets. Besides the parade, many St. Louisans fondly remembered a public school field trip to downtown's levee to see Lindbergh. "The streetcars lined up on South Broadway in front of Monroe School," Baudissin recalled. "After we got on the streetcars, the cars picked up the children from Shepard School, that was our rival school." The streetcars took them to Wharf Street (now Leonor K. Sullivan Boulevard). "Grade school students from all over the city were there. We covered the levee. Then Lindbergh flew over in the *Spirit of St. Louis*, and we all waved to him."[26]

Thousands of police kept a path clear through the half million cheering St. Louisans welcoming aviator Charles Lindbergh on June 18, 1927. He was escorted by Mayor Victor Miller in the parade celebrating Lindbergh's transforming trans-atlantic flight in his plane, the *Spirit of St. Louis*.

St. Louis businessmen funded the building of Lindbergh's unusual single-engine plane that Lindbergh himself had designed. The bells of Christ Church Cathedral peeled when news arrived that Lindbergh had safely made the 3,600-mile flight from New York to Paris in the *Spirit of St. Louis*.

Carondelet teenager Bill Dunphy had a job carrying water up to the riveters working on a high-rise. As the young Irishmen was climbing, one of the workmen yelled, "Look, that's Lindbergh." They looked up and started waving at the aviator. When Lindbergh saw them waving, "he flew down lower and waved his wings back and forth. He was so low that I felt I could reach up and touch the plane and when it passed, I could smell the fumes from the *Spirit of St. Louis*."[27]

"When I first saw the Ambassador Theatre in 1927, it was shiny and brand-spanking new. It was the most gorgeous thing I had ever seen," said lifelong South St. Louisan Frank Lafser. With its marble stairs, bronze railings, beveled mirrors, and Spanish-style chandeliers, thirteen-year-old Frank was convinced that the building on the northwest corner of Seventh and Locust Streets, "had to be one of the most beautiful theaters in the entire world."

*Two years later, Frank was an apprentice optometrist in the Dolph Building across the street from the Ambassador. The apprentice optometrists "were on the third floor. The dressing room of the Ambassadorables (the theater's chorus girls) was on the second floor. There were no curtains or shades in their windows. Every two and one-half hours they would change. We had it timed. We would all go to the windows, watch them change, then go back to work. It was amazing that we didn't break more."[28]*

A WPA poster encourages workplace safety.

The Municipal Auditorium, later named Kiel Auditorium and later renamed the Peabody Opera House, was built as part of the Memorial Plaza development. Its steel frame was covered with Indiana limestone. The auditorium measured 333 feet wide and 493 feet long, encompassing an entire city block.

In a couple of years, the Great Depression overwhelmed the nation. With the stock market crash of October 29, 1929, the nation's economy spiraled down. Building projects choked or stalled as the economy kept shrinking. The excitement, the glory, and the hoopla around Lindbergh's flight grew in people's memories as the hardships of the Depression worsened.

By March 1933, when Franklin Delano Roosevelt was inaugurated president, millions of Americans had seen their jobs disappear and their savings evaporate in runs on banks. To provide useful work for millions, Roosevelt initiated dozens of programs, including the Works Progress Administration (WPA). One of the unemployed St. Louisans who found a job with the WPA was Bohemian-born American metalworker Josef Sedlak. The Soulard resident crafted metal grills on the new Municipal Auditorium (now the Peabody Opera House).

WPA projects grouped around the new Memorial Plaza that connected Twelfth Street to Union Station added a whole new dimension to downtown St. Louis. These structures were of light gray stone. Their streamlined columns (some with convex fluting instead of concave fluting),

Mayor Victor Miller smiles at the laying of the cornerstone of the Municipal Auditorium facing Market Street at Fourteenth Street. Construction of the Municipal Auditorium, with theaters and exhibition space, provided work for craftsmen with one hundred construction firms.

geometric designs in relief, and geometric designs in grills and ornament all reflected the art deco movement. The modern Municipal Auditorium built in 1934, a new and larger Federal Court and Custom House built in 1935, and the new post office built in 1937 stirred civic pride.

The impact of these buildings was magnified because they were grouped near the fourteen-story Civil Courts Building, finished in 1930, and the impressive Soldiers' Memorial that was dedicated in 1938. The surrounding plaza created an expansive, green setting for the new buildings while visually linking them to the existing St. Louis Public Library, St. Louis City Hall, and the gray stone Municipal Courts Building.

Mayor Victor Miller breaking ground for the Civil Courts Building at Market and Twelfth Streets.

The skeleton of the Civil Courts Building rises fourteen stories, above the stone-faced lower floors, in 1928.

*When playwright Tennessee Williams returned home from his third year at the University of Missouri, his father informed him that he could no longer afford to keep him in college. Instead, he got him a job at the International Shoe Company, where he worked from 1931 to 1934. Williams later explained his pay, $65 a month, saying simply, "It was the depression." In his memoirs, Williams recalled what he had learned working at the company located at 1500 Washington Avenue, and later he described his Saturdays spent in downtown.*

"Still, I learned a lot there about the comradeship between co-workers at minimal salary, and I made some very good friends, especially a Polish fellow named Eddie, who sort of took me under his wing, and a girl named Doretta, with whom Eddie was infatuated. Then there was the spinster at the desk next to mine, little plump Nora. While we worked we carried on whispered conversations about the good movies and stage shows in town and the radio shows such as 'Amos and Andy.'

"I had Saturday afternoons off from my job. . . . I had an unvarying regime for those lovely times of release. I would go to the Mercantile Library, far downtown in St. Louis, and read voraciously there; I would have a thirty-five-cent lunch at a pleasant little restaurant. And I would go home in a 'service car.'"[29]

Luther Ely Smith, shown in his office, spearheaded the campaign to create the Jefferson National Expansion Memorial on the riverfront.

While the clean lines of these new, light-colored stone buildings were reshaping the Memorial Plaza area of western downtown, the riverfront was the front door to visitors arriving by train. A few Bohemian artists and nightclubs took advantage of the cheap rents and enjoyed the romance of the mid-nineteenth-century warehouses along the narrow cobblestone streets of the riverfront. The blocks of underused or vacant warehouses, however, looked dirty and neglected, and some civic leaders decided to erase the decaying warehouse district to create a new entrance for St. Louis.

A campaign began in 1933 to establish a riverfront memorial honoring Thomas Jefferson for his vision of an expansive United States. The memorial would also recognize the role this riverfront acreage had as the Gateway to the West. Local attorney and civic leader Luther Ely Smith proposed

In 1931, with the ranks of the unemployed swelling, out-of-work St. Louisans marched in downtown to bring attention to their plight.

that the memorial cover thirty-seven blocks stretching south from the Eads Bridge.

Despite the hardships of the Great Depression, the citizens of St. Louis passed a $7,500,000 bond issue to pay for the creation of a great memorial. The WPA would fund the rest of the cost.

Five hundred buildings, many constructed with ornamental cast-iron facades, were razed. The very buildings that had served as the machinery of westward expansion were wiped off the site to create a monument to what they had powered. Demolition began only weeks after Nazi Germany invaded Poland, beginning World War II. While the nation and the city turned their eyes toward battles in the Pacific and in

Emerson Electric workers in the coil winding department on Washington Avenue. Organized in 1890, the company moved to the 2000 block of Washington Avenue in 1903. In 1920, the company constructed an eight-story factory at 2020 Washington.

Emerson workers at the grinding machines in their plant at 2020 Washington. The company produced electric fans and small motors for household appliances. After the attack on Pearl Harbor, the company converted its production to armaments.

Dated 1944, this motivational poster reads as a prayer.

Ladies' Auxiliary No. 66 of the United Automobile Workers marching on Twelfth Street as part of the Labor Day parade of 1938.

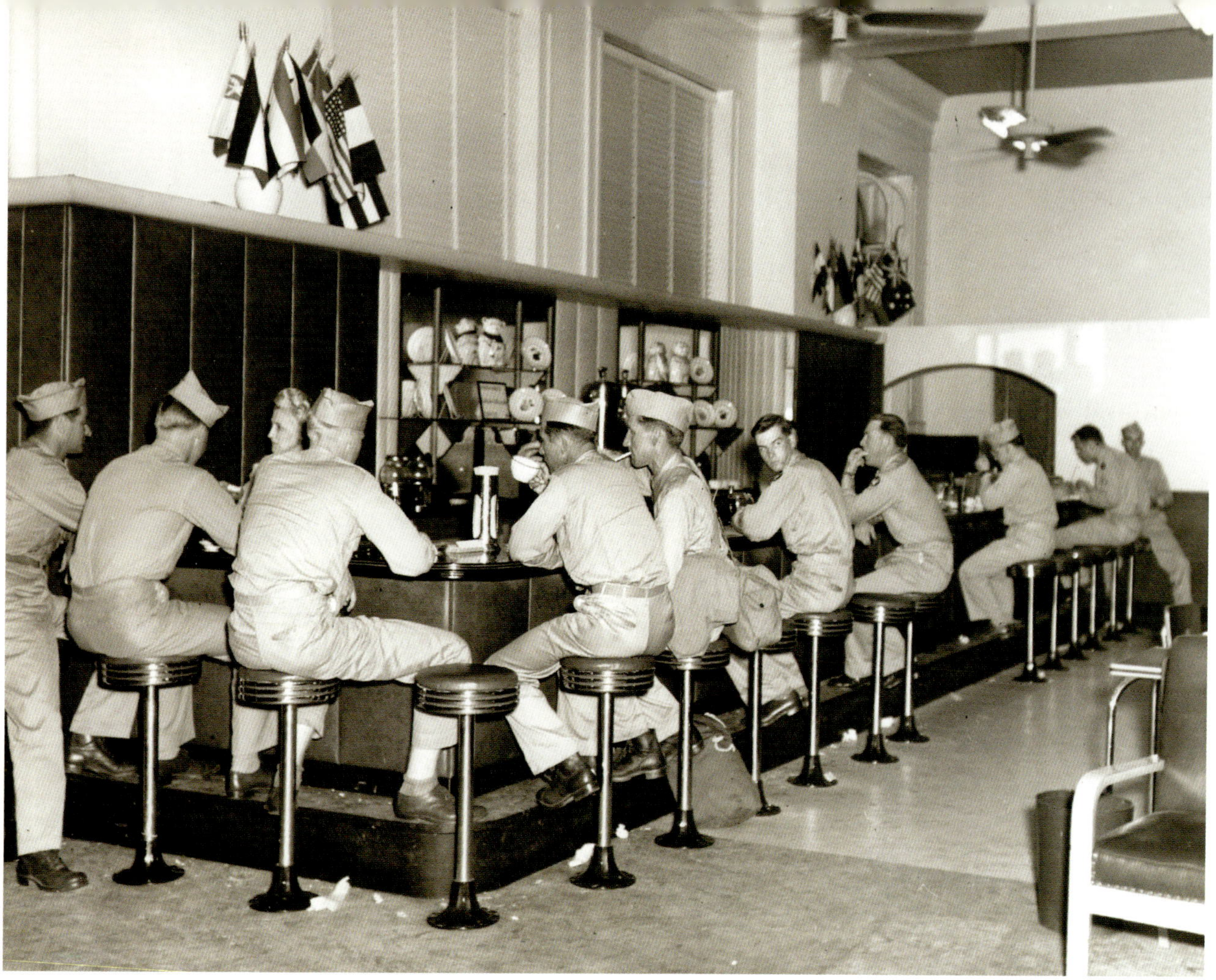

![photo]

This 1943 scene of men in uniform at the coffee shop at Union Station was repeated daily at diners and eateries throughout downtown, as St. Louis served as a transfer point and oasis for servicemen en route to military posts and camps across the nation and overseas.

Europe, the riverfront was left with empty blocks waiting for a monument.

The Monday morning after the Japanese attacked Pearl Harbor, lines of volunteers were waiting for the doors to open at the armed forces recruiting offices in the new Federal Building at Market and Twelfth Streets. That day, the day that Franklin Delano Roosevelt addressed Congress and war was declared on Japan, St. Louisans went to work to defeat the Axis. Eventually, two hundred thousand St. Louisans were employed in war plants.

To save fabric for the war effort, the garment industry on Washington Avenue introduced new fashion lines that eliminated cuffs, hoods, and trim, and shortened skirts. The garment businesses, however, focused their new, long hours on manufacturing uniforms, battle jackets, military caps, parachutes, and field tents. International Shoe and St. Louis's other shoe manufacturers converted production from high heels and dress shoes to put out millions of military boots and shoes. In Emerson Electric's factory at 2020 Washington Avenue, laborers, craftsmen, and engineers constructed parts for the gun turrets for the B-17 Flying Fortress and the B-24 Liberator heavy bombers.

St. Louis's medical suppliers turned their energies toward the war effort. The St. Louis Army Medical Depot was located in the Mart Building with its twenty-

*An American soldier stationed in India wrote in thanks for the kindness shown him at the downtown USO (United Service Organization). The Star-Times published the letter on February 3, 1944, as part of an article celebrating the work of the local USO.*

"When I came to St. Louis I guess I was pretty fed up with army life, but as soon as I arrived there I felt way inside me a feeling I was no longer an outsider, a person coming in to put more burden on a town!—but accepted as one of the family. It amazed me to see not one or two people, but all the people in St. Louis were the same—always willing to help and make a soldier feel right at home. . . . Well, all I can say is that when I came to India I thought sure enough I would give it all up, and that I just wouldn't be able to take it. Then came St. Louis, the people in it, the Kiel Auditorium U.S.O. and all those friends I had made there, and I knew if I'd fall down here, it would make a poor showing, considering all they did for me. So I put my teeth together and stuck my chin out 'cause I certainly was not going to let people down, especially those who did not leave me down when I needed it."[30]

A volunteer appears to stash treats in the backpack of a World War II soldier boarding a troop train at Union Station.

Color guard for the Armistice Day parade of 1944 marching west on Chestnut Street.

five acres of floor space. In this building, field hospitals were equipped and shipped on the adjacent rails to serve battlefields around the globe.

Seventy-five percent of St. Louis industries were involved in manufacturing war materials. But tens of thousands of young soldiers, airmen, and sailors did not equate St. Louis with the landing craft produced here, or the parts for planes and gliders manufactured here, or the cartridges made at the huge arms plant, or with our stove and pipe companies that switched to producing bomb casings. For those young Americans, St. Louis was the welcome they received at the USO.

Union Station was the portal for Jefferson Barracks, Fort Leonard Wood, and Scott Air Force Base. And thousands of young soldiers being deployed were passing through St. Louis. Civic leaders and regular citizens were prepared to host the young servicemen. They had dedicated the downtown USO center in the Municipal Auditorium in July 1941.

Private Edward J. Smith praised the work conducted at the downtown USO. "In my opinion, which is shared by thousands of other soldiers, St. Louis is a real service man's town."

"The basement of the Municipal Auditorium has been turned over to the USO. This spacious area is a scene of daily activity: dances, hobbies, information, sleeping quarters, lounge, literature, etc., and a visiting service man can always find an invitation for some kind of entertainment."

"Here's where the people of St. Louis shine: Churches, clubs, families and individuals are always planning dances, suppers, parties, shows, etc. They even call the USO in their cars or cabs and take the boys to the scene of events."[31]

By Christmas of 1944, the downtown USO center had hosted three million guests.

The factories were working three shifts, the

This image of soldiers in World War I uniforms are molded into the aluminum elevator doors at the Soldiers' Memorial.

streetcars were full, and lines were at the movie houses and department store perfume counters. The people who worked in the stores, the factories, and the offices of downtown St. Louis, however, were focused on the newspaper and radio bulletins of news from Europe and the Pacific.

   At 8:36 a.m. on Monday, May 7, 1945, KSD radio broadcast that the Germans had unconditionally surrendered. The announcement was almost the sole topic of conversation on downtown streets and on streetcars and buses. At Seventh and Olive Streets, two soldiers referring to the defeat of Italy and Germany swapped such remarks as "Two down, one to go" and "We still have the Japs to lick."

A listening policeman said, "That's right, only half done now." A young woman at Broadway and Olive said, "Wonderful. Almost too good to be true. My brother's in Germany and my husband in the Pacific."[32]

The expectation of months, perhaps years, more of war, of moving battle-weary troops from Europe to the war in the Pacific, and of continuing shortages and rationing all suddenly ended. The dropping of the atomic bombs on Hiroshima and Nagasaki brought an abrupt end to Japan's resolve.

During the wee hours of August 14, 1945, a noisy caravan of merrymakers, honking horns, and ringing bells passed along Franklin Avenue. Their celebration woke sleeping residents who had been unaware of reports of Japan's surrender. Just after daylight, the doors of St. John the Apostle Church and Christ Church Cathedral were opened for worshippers. News bulletins sent a wave of rejoicing through downtown. Teenagers erupted in a spontaneous snake dance on Olive Street in front of the Old Post Office, the center of downtown partying. Vendors selling flags and noisemakers gathered there. The honking of automobile horns and the clattering of tin cans tied to fenders filled the air. Downtown sidewalks were littered with ticker tape. The dominant note was, "Now the boys will be coming home!"[33]

Joe E. Brown, comedian of vaudeville and early film, sits with a 1934 Cardinal player at a game.

---

*Custom tailor James Feeney, a veteran baseball major leaguer, opened his tailor shop at 415 Chestnut Street in 1912. With visits from his baseball buddies and a billiard table in the back room, the shop became home to the hot stove league each winter. In a 1954 interview, Joe E. Brown (1891–1973), comic star of early movies, reminisced about his early days in vaudeville when he used to visit Feeney's tailor shop.*

"I've always loved coming to St. Louis. You could always get in a baseball argument here and there's nothing I'd rather do than talk about baseball. And you can't talk about it without arguing about it.

"In the old days of vaudeville, Feeney's on Ninth Street, right across from the Orpheum Theater, was the place to go. You'd always find players or umpires or managers or just plain fans in there arguing. I remember there used to be a policeman on duty there on Ninth who told people to keep moving whenever they passed Feeney's. 'If you don't,' he would say, 'you're liable to get hit by a foul tip.'"[34]

The monumental Milles fountain, the work of Swedish sculptor Carl Milles, was completed in 1939. Its prominent location, Aloe Plaza opposite the entrance to Union Station, was a link in the Memorial Plaza. The fountain's fourteen figures celebrate the confluence of the Mississippi and Missouri Rivers. The main figures of the fountain were considered so provocative that it caused a stir. To calm the concerns, the official name was changed from *Wedding of the Rivers* to *Meeting of the Waters*.

a. Crowds outside Lipic's, the pen house of St. Louis, during the 1943 Christmas season.

b. Men in straw hats fill the sidewalk in front of the Chemical Building.

c. Interior of a downtown barber shop in 1924.

d. Thomas Rizzo produce stand in Union Market, circa 1919.

e. Flying Circus pilot Charles Fowler sweeps in front of the Railway Exchange Building with his wife, Marie Meyer, on the wings of his biplane during the summer of 1924.

A 1959 scene of shoppers on the first floor of Stix, Baer and Fuller department store at Washington Avenue and Seventh Street.

## Chapter 5

# 1945–PRESENT

Henry Changar sold appliances at Stix, Baer and Fuller in downtown St. Louis. His strong accent revealed that he was a native of Warsaw, Poland; his last name was originally spelled Ciezar. His whole family had been killed at Auschwitz. A teenager at the time, Henry had escaped when he was being loaded into cattle cars headed for the camp. Later, he was imprisoned at the Treblinka death camp. When the war ended, he settled in St. Louis where his uncle Morris was his sponsor. He built a new life here, marrying Shirley and eventually getting a job selling large appliances at Stix, Baer and Fuller in downtown St. Louis. Working on commission, he built a ranch house in Creve Coeur. Wearing his uniform suit and tie, he drove an old, maroon-colored Chevy with bubble-shaped bumpers to the department store. He carried a can of oil with him at all times because the car leaked so much oil. Henry often drove the old Chevy to the homes of customers to show them how to use the state-of-the-art dishwasher or how to set the temperature in their new refrigerator.[35]

Downtown St. Louis survived the challenges of the last half of the twentieth century—competition posed by the new American dream of the suburban ranch house, industrial parks, and suburban malls—to experience a renaissance at the beginning of the twenty-first century. After losing industries and some corporate headquarters, this rebirth took a radically different course. It was built on old-fashioned, walkable downtown neighborhoods set amidst St. Louis's extraordinary historic brick, granite, and terra-cotta architecture mixed in with sleek glass-and-steel skyscrapers.

A Famous-Barr window display from Christmas 1979.

Christmas lights strung across the streets of downtown.

The path from the street celebrations at the news of the victory in World War II to this reincarnation of downtown, with residents walking their dogs as they go to their favorite coffeehouse on a Saturday morning, was not direct. Development in downtown suffered slumps as well as surges of renewed energy.

In the autumn of 1945, a joyous mood filled the streets of downtown. In that first holiday season after the war, the enormous Famous-Barr department store at Sixth and Olive Streets bustled as hundreds of extra employees helped handle the Christmas rush. In the midst of the holiday commotion, the staff of Famous-Barr conducted the sixth annual Christmas party for disabled and underprivileged children. Five thousand boys and girls from thirty institutions, representing every creed and race, flocked to the ninth floor auditorium for the party. The auditorium was decorated with a circus theme. Santa Claus and his troupe of clowns entertained the parade of children for five hours.

The party was broadcast over KXOK radio, as volunteers from the young audience led sing-alongs of Christmas carols.

With the optimism and confidence of postwar America, St. Louisans returned to the task of building a memorial to the optimism of the Louisiana Purchase and to the optimism of the explorers, soldiers, miners, and farmers who began their journey to build new lives on the St. Louis riverfront.

Civic leaders held a competition for American architects to design an inspiring riverfront memorial. St. Louisans privately raised the huge sum of $225,000 for prize money. Coast to coast, architects started dreaming of statues, buildings, symbols, and shapes that could grace the St. Louis levee. The designs, like the evolving culture, were futuristic. Of the 172 entries, one was unlike all the rest in its simplicity, its beauty, and its symbolism. Eero Saarinen's Gateway Arch, a triangular ribbon of gleaming steel forming a graceful arch reaching to the clouds, was chosen for the memorial. Though relocating railroads and financing the huge project

A young girl roams amongst shelves of board games in the toy department of Stix, Baer and Fuller department store in 1959.

Shirley Changar got a sales job at Stix, Baer and Fuller downtown, in "Girls' Wear 7 through 14." She and her husband, Henry, drove downtown together. When they couldn't find a babysitter, they took their three children with them. Young Glenn, Murray, and Carla loved the commotion at Christmastime. They would spend the day riding the monorail that hung from the ceiling over the toy department, or looking at the store windows with moving Santas. Sometimes the children explored the back stairs where old mannequins were stored.[36]

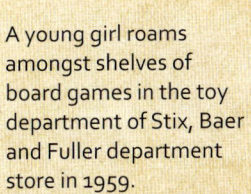

delayed construction for years, the creation of the Gateway Arch had begun.

Downtown was returning to a peacetime economy. The garment industry boomed with the end of fabric rationing. St. Louis was the Paris of the juniors and misses apparel trade, and Washington Avenue was the street for the industry. For many displaced persons from war-ravaged Europe, their first step to building a new life in America was getting a job on Washington Avenue. American troops had liberated Oscar Ozarowski and his fellow prisoners from the Wobbelin concentration

Pavers form a zipper pattern down the center of Washington Avenue, recalling that the impressive architecture filled with fashionable condominiums and apartments once housed the old garment district.

Immediately following World War II, the St. Louis garment industry boomed. As late as 1967, twelve thousand St. Louisans were working in the industry, producing everything from lingerie to millinery to bridal gowns.

camp. After three years in a displaced persons camp, the native of Poland was able to immigrate to the United States. Eventually, he moved to St. Louis and got a job as a tailor making overcoats for the Modern Jacket Company in the Merchandise Mart at 1000 Washington Avenue. (He supported his wife, Eva Buchbleter, whom he met at a Jewish picnic, and their children through his work at Modern Jacket until his retirement in 1977.)[37]

In 1960 the St. Louis Chamber of Commerce reported that the city ranked sixth in the nation as an apparel producing center. Employees in local textile and apparel manufacturers numbered fifteen thousand.

Downtown was a working neighborhood, but the residential character had virtually disappeared in the early years of the twentieth century. Civic leaders decided to rebuild an apartment community in downtown St. Louis. In preparation, the headache balls cleared everything but the churches from Fifteenth to Seventeenth between

Girl Scout leaders wave goodbye before boarding a train at Union Station.

Contestants in the Miss Downtown St. Louis competition of 1964.

Children enjoy a walk around the Milles fountain in 1960. The backdrop is the head house for Union Station, which stretches two full city blocks along Market Street.

At noontime, masses of workers mobbed the streets, window shopping, stopping at a bank, or going to Baker's Shoes on their way to a diner or coffee shop.

Plaza Square Apartments were constructed around two churches, Centenary Methodist Church dating to 1871 and St. John the Baptist Church built in 1860, as the historic setting for the apartment development.

Once completed, the stunningly modern Plaza Square Apartments offered 156 two-bedroom units, 600 one-bedroom units, and 334 efficiency apartments for rent.

Chestnut and Olive Streets. Plaza Square, six shiny new apartment towers that housed 1,090 units, were built on the site. Porcelain-enamel panels, colored in shades of turquoise, coral, and yellow highlighted these pale brick towers and gave them a stunning midcentury modern style.

With the 1960s enthusiasm for the new and modern, so often at the expense of the historic, writer Robert Paul Jordan described the changes he witnessed in downtown St. Louis for *National Geographic* magazine. In 1965 he wrote about the scale of the transformation west of Twelfth Street: "Wherever I looked, [the headache ball] was smashing the ribs of weary hotels, grimy warehouses, sagging tenements. . . .

"I shook my head, awed. I remembered the smoke stained old river town fondly from World War II days, a haven to me and thousands of other servicemen on weekend passes from nearby bases. Now, after more than 20 years, I had returned to a St. Louis I never knew. . . .

The promenade of the Mansion House complex hosted events and sculpture exhibits. In 1967, part of the promenade was used as a putting green.

"St. Louis tackled the blight that has beset most American cities: slums, traffic congestion, stagnation. Today the old river town rips out decrepit buildings by the block. In their place rise urban-renewal projects such as colorful Plaza Square Apartments on Memorial Plaza."[38]

The obstacles to building the Gateway Arch—funding, railroad tracks, even the Korean War—had been removed or concluded. The nitty-gritty of building the Arch began with removing three hundred thousand cubic feet of earth and rock for the foundation and underground museum. Workers poured twenty-six thousand tons of concrete for the foundation of the Arch. Craftsmen set in place the first stainless steel section on February 12, 1963. To ensure the stability of the 630-foot monument, each wall of the Arch was built like a sandwich, with concrete poured between an outer skin and an interior wall. At ground level, a cross-section of each leg measured fifty-four feet wide. Gradually, the legs grew more and more slender as they rose. At the top of the Arch, the legs would measure only seventeen feet wide.

As work progressed and the Arch was reaching for the sky, the mid-air

Beginning in 1940, the streamlined *Admiral* docked on the riverfront where floating palaces had docked during the nineteenth century. The biggest excursion steamboat ever built, the art deco *Admiral* boasted five decks and measured 375 feet long.

construction site became more and more hazardous. Monday through Friday, scores of skilled ironworkers, welders, electricians, machine operators, concrete men, pipe fitters, and sheet metal specialists worked in the sky over the historic riverfront. At dizzying heights, whipped by the wind, the hard hats welded the huge triangles together with their strength and skill.

On October 28, 1965, St. Louisans were mesmerized. Ten thousand watched from the Arch grounds, thousands more watched from downtown office buildings and warehouses, and the rest of St. Louis watched on television, as the skilled workers seemed to effortlessly slip the keystone into the top of the stainless steel arch.

The Arch was higher than the Washington Monument and 175 feet higher than the Statue of Liberty. It surpassed all other American monuments and rivaled the great monuments of the world. It framed the St. Louis skyline, making it unlike any other.

After nearly a century of downtown activity moving away from the riverfront, the construction of the

The completed Gateway Arch drew St. Louisans like a magnet as the memorial's grounds served as the setting for ethnic festivals, runs, and concerts.

Lifelong South St. Louisan Billie Baudissin took the Gravois bus, Number 10, to work at the offices of Edison Brothers Shoes her entire working career. Their offices filled the eight-story building at Fourth and Washington. On the morning of October 28, 1965, everybody in her office quit work. They crowded around the windows, looking through binoculars, waiting to see the final stainless steel triangle, the keystone, put in place to complete the Gateway Arch.

"People thought it would take days to fit it together. They were taking bets on how long it would take!" As a giant crane lifted the keystone the 360 feet to the narrow gap at the top of the Arch, men were hosing down the legs of the Arch with firehoses. They were trying to keep the stainless steel from expanding with the heat of the day. If the steel expanded too much, they wouldn't be able to fit in the keystone. As the keystone got nearer and nearer the top of the Arch, the tension built.

"Then it went together just like that," Billie said. Cheers erupted through the office. It was one of the world's architectural wonders. "But everybody at work was disappointed," she remembered. "We thought that we would be able to kill more time."[39]

Gateway Arch acted as a magnet, pulling energy and development toward the river. Busch Stadium, the first downtown home for the St. Louis Baseball Cardinals, was constructed simultaneously with the Arch. Its design had been an issue. Jack Sverdrup, the great engineer of Sverdrup and Parcel, was set to design and build the stadium. The general who had built roads in Burmese jungles and airfields in the South Pacific where the Japanese could not intended the new downtown stadium to be his St. Louis project or his own "memorial."[40] Civic leader Howard F. Baer felt this major project needed an architect. At a regular monthly meeting of Civic Progress, Baer made a plea for a good architectural design for something so important to the city. In response, Gussie Busch rose to his feet.

"Howard is right. I've got $5 million of Busch money in this thing. When my grandchildren walk around this town, they ought to be proud of it. Get an architect!"[41]

Architect Edward Durell Stone designed and Jack Sverdrup built the coliseum-style Busch Stadium. A series of graceful arches, echoing the Gateway Arch itself, ringed the roof of the new stadium.

After the Cardinals-Giants game on May 8, 1966, a band led the seventeen thousand fans at old Sportsman's Park on North Grand in singing "Auld Lang Syne." The groundskeeper pried up home plate and carried it by helicopter to the new stadium.

The round, coliseum-style Busch Stadium, part of an eighty-two-acre redevelopment west of the memorial grounds, was built simultaneously with the Gateway Arch.

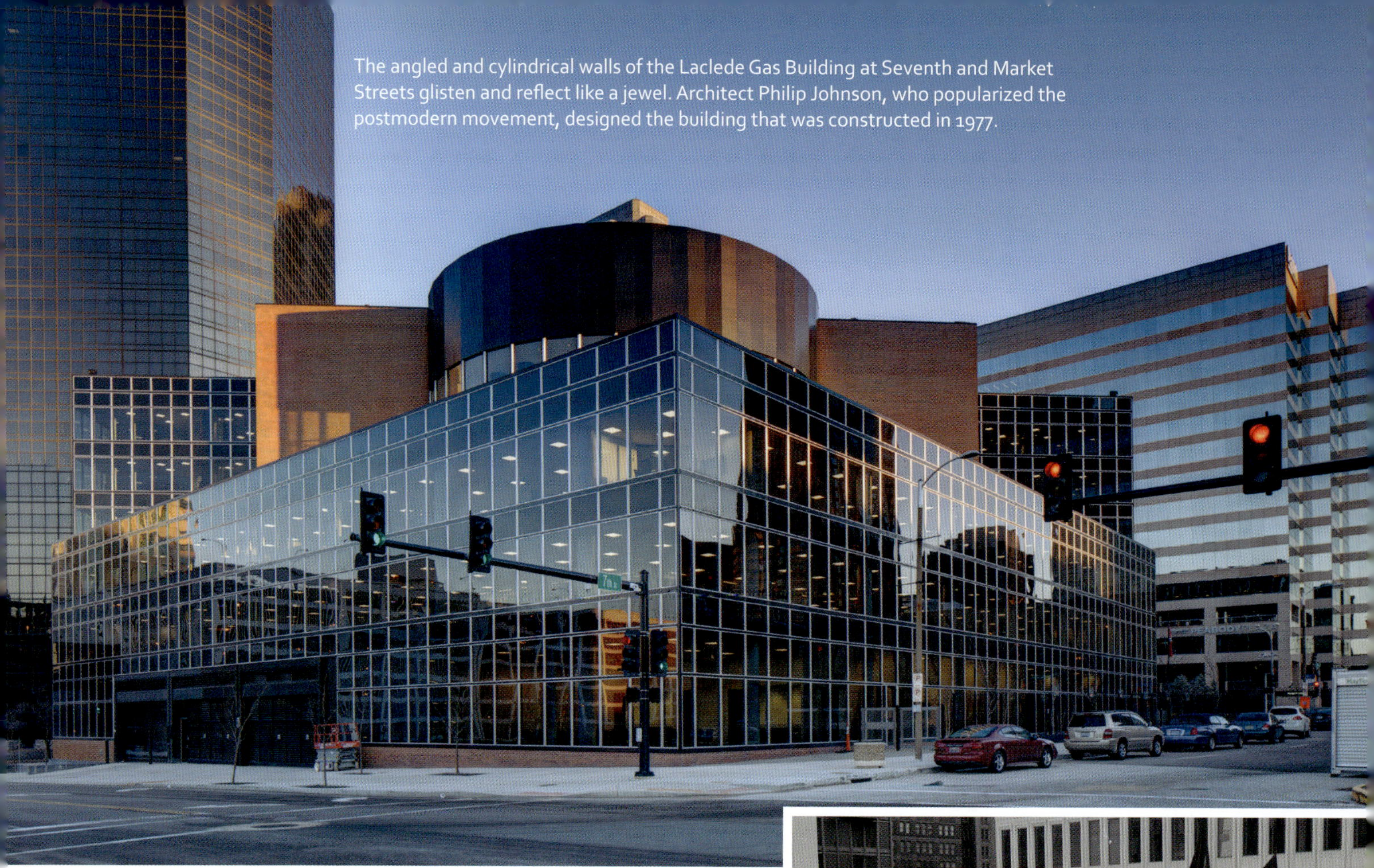

The angled and cylindrical walls of the Laclede Gas Building at Seventh and Market Streets glisten and reflect like a jewel. Architect Philip Johnson, who popularized the postmodern movement, designed the building that was constructed in 1977.

The new stadium covered twelve acres and seated more than fifty-three thousand fans for baseball games. Its curving ramps and rooftop arches gave it distinctively graceful lines.

During the 1960s and 1970s, steel, concrete, and glass monuments to the International Style punctuated the skyline of downtown. Their sleek walls that seemed to shoot into the clouds contrasted with downtown's ornate brick and terracotta skyscrapers that were topped by embellished cornices or stepped setbacks. The Mansion House, three towers rising from a raised promenade, provided a modern-style backdrop for the Gateway Arch. The Gateway Tower at One Memorial Drive, the glass and steel surfaces of the Boatmen's Tower, and the Equitable Building reflecting its neighboring Old Courthouse all created a new, modern skyline that was like a set for the space-age Gateway Arch.

A live television show was staged on the Mansion House promenade in 1972.

Then, in the 1980s, the fanciful building profiles of the postmodernism movement, like the stepped roofline of One Bell Center, once again reshaped the skyline. For its design of One Bell Center, St. Louis's Hellmuth, Obata & Kassabaum was inspired by the adjacent art deco–style 1010 Pine building constructed almost sixty years earlier. The firm topped the Edison Brothers Stores Building with a series of arches. (The building is now home to Stifel, Nicolaus & Co.) Hellmuth, Obata & Kassabaum crowned their forty-two-story granite-and-glass Metropolitan Square Building with steeply pitched, green-gabled roofs reminiscent of a French chateau.

While each new office building added another facet to downtown, many giant, beautifully crafted turn-of-the-century buildings were left vacant or underutilized as industries closed or left downtown. The once thriving garment industry was shrinking. Where busy laborers had conversed in a half a dozen

A Mansion House get-together on the promenade in 1979.

HOK's design for the Stifel, Nicolaus & Co. building at Broadway and Washington Avenue celebrated the postmodern movement with its playful row of arches at the roofline.

languages, voices echoed, and the streets were empty. The huge warehouses were vulnerable. On April 2, 1976, a firestorm swept through the western edge of downtown, turning buildings to rubble and leaving gaping holes in the building scape.

The headache ball threatened civic treasures in downtown's core, but it also stirred civic outrage and inspired the incipient preservation movement. Citizens rallied to prevent the razing of the Old Post Office for parking. After protests halted plans to raze Laclede's Landing, the Raeder Building, with its ornate Victorian-era cast-iron facade, and other riverfront warehouses underwent massive renovations. In 1985 the renovation of Union Station as a hotel, marketplace, and conference center was the largest renovation project accomplished in the nation. The city of St. Louis led the nation in historic rehabs.

In 1986 historic rehabilitation "came to a grinding halt in the city," according to Jerry Schlichter, a plaintiff attorney with offices in downtown. Tax reform had severely curtailed credits for renovating historic buildings.

Built in 1874, the Raeder Building on Laclede's Landing boasts a spectacular, six-story cast-iron facade. It was painstakingly restored in 1980.

The graceful cast-iron columns on the interior of the Old Post Office at Eighth and Olive Streets. After historic preservationists defeated repeated attempts to raze the Old Post Office for a parking garage, the building was renovated for office and commercial space.

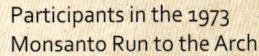

The Miss Downtown St. Louis parade of 1974.

Participants in the 1973 Monsanto Run to the Arch.

"People don't realize it, but we almost lost the city of St. Louis," said Deputy Fire Chief Louis Stauss, describing the firestorm that consumed warehouses in the western part of downtown on Friday, April 2, 1976. Scrap metal thieves using an acetylene torch ignited a fire in a seven-story warehouse at Locust and Twenty-First Streets. When the firemen arrived, flames engulfed the building and were spreading rapidly to other buildings.

The magnitude of the fire became so great that it created its own wind velocity. The heat of the inferno sucked in the air, and shot it upward. The winds of the firestorm were literally blowing down firemen on Washington Avenue, a block away. The winds even deflected the pressurized streams of water.

Almost all the city's firemen and equipment, more than two hundred men and fifty-one fire trucks, were fighting the blaze. At this point, Fire Chief Charles R. Kamprad considered using dynamite. "Fortunately, it never came to that," Kamprad related. "I can only credit the supreme effort of the fire fighters who moved in close—within 25 feet—to get water into the inferno. They were moving in at a time when spectators were moving two blocks away to escape the heat."[42]

When the firemen finally suppressed the fire, the flames had destroyed six buildings on Locust Street and extensively damaged one on Locust Street, two on Olive Street, and one on Washington Avenue. Though the St. Louis Fire Department conquered the fierce flames, the firestorm left gaps in the western edge of downtown.

The grand opening of Schnucks Culinaria at Ninth and Olive Streets in 2009 marked the return of downtown as a residential neighborhood. The Culinaria's immediate neighborhood, Old Post Office Square, has seen the reinvention of the office district as a high-rise residential community with apartments in the Paul Brown, Arcade, Wright, and Syndicate Trust Buildings.

Schlichter explained, "the numbers simply don't work for rehab for rent or for sale without incentives." He made it his personal mission "to create an incentive to turn those derelict buildings—which could be our best asset—into what they would become if they could be rehabbed."[43]

Schlichter "first made four trips to Washington to see if there would be any interest in reviving the federal credit as it was." When he found no appetite for it, "I wrote a [state] bill, modeled after the federal law. It had to be more friendly for development, more user-friendly, so that is the way I wrote it. . . . I wanted to just walk the hallways of the capital in my spare time and ask people to sponsor it. So I did."[44]

Schlichter's legislation, which came online in 1998, sparked a boom in historic renovation in downtown. Warehouses that had served the tobacco, shoe, or dry goods industries were adapted for the twenty-first century. These huge historic warehouses featuring rough-cut granite, terra-cotta arches, and sculptural cornices were transformed into stylish apartments and condos. From the Romanesque-style Merchandise Mart Building at 1000 Washington Avenue to the World War I–era Emerson Electric Building at 2020 Washington Avenue, a remarkable neighborhood developed. Office buildings around the Old Post Office at Eighth and Olive Streets

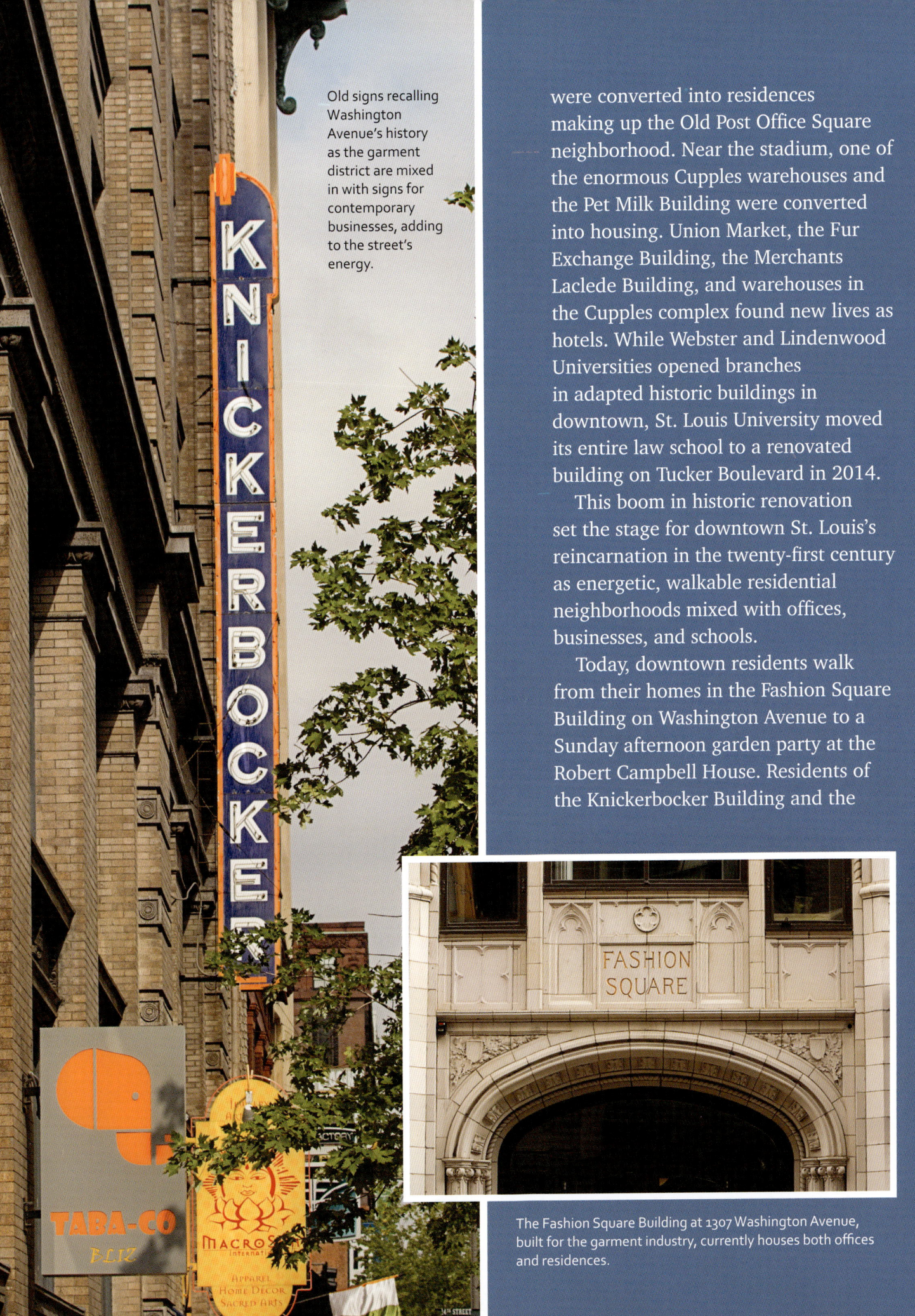

Old signs recalling Washington Avenue's history as the garment district are mixed in with signs for contemporary businesses, adding to the street's energy.

were converted into residences making up the Old Post Office Square neighborhood. Near the stadium, one of the enormous Cupples warehouses and the Pet Milk Building were converted into housing. Union Market, the Fur Exchange Building, the Merchants Laclede Building, and warehouses in the Cupples complex found new lives as hotels. While Webster and Lindenwood Universities opened branches in adapted historic buildings in downtown, St. Louis University moved its entire law school to a renovated building on Tucker Boulevard in 2014.

This boom in historic renovation set the stage for downtown St. Louis's reincarnation in the twenty-first century as energetic, walkable residential neighborhoods mixed with offices, businesses, and schools.

Today, downtown residents walk from their homes in the Fashion Square Building on Washington Avenue to a Sunday afternoon garden party at the Robert Campbell House. Residents of the Knickerbocker Building and the

The Fashion Square Building at 1307 Washington Avenue, built for the garment industry, currently houses both offices and residences.

Century-old Cupples Station warehouse buildings have been converted into an hotel and another into apartments. Originally praised for their efficient connection to railroad tunnels and spur lines, their lasting appeal is due to their elegant design featuring red brick arches and corbelled cornices.

Located in a Richardsonian Romanesque building constructed for Bell Telephone in 1889, Baileys' Range specializes in old-fashioned burgers and shakes and caters to locals and tourists, from kids to seniors.

Cupples warehouses regularly meet at a pickup chess game at Washington Avenue Post at 1315 Washington Avenue. On wintry Saturday mornings, residents from the Syndicate Trust Building walk across Tenth Street for coffee and gooey butter cake at Park Avenue Coffee. On a summer Saturday afternoon, sunbathers surround the rooftop wading pool at the Paul Brown Building. A retired U.S. Air Force couple, who have lived downtown for nine years, explain that they gave up their car as an unnecessary expense since they walk to the grocery, the hair salon, the dentist, the weekly noontime

From childhood, native St. Louisan Dustin Bopp was passionate about St. Louis's great architecture. As an architect, Bopp has been instrumental in redesigning great downtown office buildings and warehouses into residential buildings, including the Bankers Lofts, the Railway Lofts, and half a dozen others. The past president of the St. Louis Chapter of the American Institute of Architects celebrates downtown architectural wealth and its vibrant community life.

"Downtowns evolve. Fortunately, we inherited an amazing collection of substantial nineteenth- and twentieth-century buildings. Robust and artful structures that once primarily supported manufacturing and commerce have been adapted into unique contemporary homes whose residents—spanning generations—create a vibrant neighborhood. Downtown St. Louis is not just a place to visit, but to make a life."[45]

The twenty-one-story Railway Exchange Building with thirty acres of floor space was claimed to be the largest building in the world. It covered the entire city block bounded by Sixth, Seventh, Olive, and Locust Streets. Elegant, cream-colored terra-cotta with swags, corner scrolls, and sculptures of women's faces sheathed all four of the building's facades.

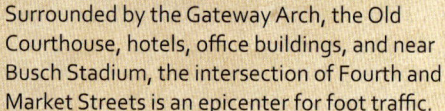

Great Rivers Greenway is developing bike trails that follow the river and hook together parks and neighborhoods with downtown and the Jefferson National Expansion Memorial.

Surrounded by the Gateway Arch, the Old Courthouse, hotels, office buildings, and near Busch Stadium, the intersection of Fourth and Market Streets is an epicenter for foot traffic.

Construction of an extension of the Jefferson National Expansion Memorial grounds that will connect to Luther Ely Smith Park. The park roofs the interstate with a green sward.

Massive reconstruction redirects the new entrance to the museum under the Arch. The new entrance faces the Old Courthouse and incorporates the museum into downtown life.

A playful sculpture in Citygarden, an interactive sculpture garden filling the blocks of the Gateway Mall between Eighth and Tenth Streets. This sculpture is hollow, and visitors climb into the head to view downtown from its eyes.

concerts at Post Office Square, and the Metrolink station. By 2014 residents in the core of downtown numbered eight thousand.

While construction equipment clogs the streets as more vacant office buildings are converted into apartments, another dimension is about to enrich the character of downtown St. Louis. This time, however, it wasn't the developers or the architect or the businessmen who brought about this transformation; instead, it was the voters in the city and county of St. Louis. At the polling place, they demonstrated their commitment to downtown St. Louis when they passed CityArchRiver, a proposition in 2013 to help fund a renovation of the setting of the Gateway Arch. This is the first time in the nation's history that residents of a locality have taxed themselves to enhance a national park.

The CityArchRiver project will extend parkland over the sunken highway that has been a barrier between the Arch grounds and the rest of downtown since the monument was

Sculptural playgrounds built of architectural salvage on the roof of the City Museum. The development of the City Museum in the 1990s spurred interest in the then underutilized warehouses of Washington Avenue.

completed. This will enable the parkland to flow to the Old Courthouse, Kiener Plaza, and the core of downtown. CityArchRiver will connect the government offices, the hotels, the baseball stadium, and the new residential neighborhoods in the old garment district and surrounding the Old Post Office with the city's most historic site—the grounds of the

For two days in July 2015, a one-thousand-foot waterslide was installed down Market Street between Jefferson Avenue and Twentieth Street.

Gateway Arch, where the first St. Louisans built French pioneer houses of stone and upright logs.

Downtown St. Louis emerged from the last seven decades as a national treasure. This extraordinary downtown boasts a wealth of magnificent historic warehouses and office buildings adapted for the twenty-first century. A new generation of dramatic International Style and postmodern skyscrapers shapes the skyline. With CityArchRiver, expansive parkland will be an integral part of downtown's walkable neighborhoods, and that unique urban scenery is framed by the Gateway Arch, one of the great sculptures of the world.

Sculptures, fountains, and pools in a setting of native plantings invite children and adults to enjoy Citygarden. The garden is maintained by the Gateway Foundation.

Katie with Nick the Horse of the St. Louis Carriage Company provides a unique way to experience downtown St. Louis.

In 1964, with the Gateway Arch under construction, thousands of St. Louisans celebrated the Fourth of July on the riverfront. People spilled down the steps toward the vendor booths on Wharf Street. The building of the Arch drew development toward it. Soon the Gateway Tower, Boatmen's Tower, the cylindrical hotel tower (originally Stouffer's Riverfront), and the Mansion House complex provided a modern backdrop for the space-age monument.

a.

b.

c.

d.

a. Miss Hulling's Cafeteria, 725 Olive, 1957.
b. The courtyard atrium of the Laurel, the former Stix, Baer and Fuller department store.
c. Festival crowds on the riverfront.
d. Flying Saucer Draught Emporium in the Cupples.
e. Busch Stadium, the first downtown stadium, in early stages of construction.
f. The Thomas F. Eagleton United States Courthouse.
g. The retro Busch Stadium, designed to complement the remaining Cupples warehouses.
h. Morton D. May Amphitheater in the Gateway Mall.

# ENDNOTES

1. Gregory P. Ames, editor, *Auguste Chouteau's Journal: Memory, Mythmaking and History in the Heritage of New France* (St. Louis: St. Louis Mercantile Library, 2010), 41–96.
2. Nicolas de Finiels, *An Account of Upper Louisiana*, ed. Carl J. Ekberg and William E. Foley, trans. Carl J. Ekberg (University of Missouri Press, 1989), 69.
3. Ibid., 65.
4. Ibid., 118.
5. Timothy Flint, *Recollections of the Last Ten Years, Passed in Occasional Residences and Journeying in the Valley of the Mississippi* (Boston: Cummings, Hilliard, and Company, 1826), 110.
6. Ibid., 142.
7. John F. Darby, *Personal Recollections of John F. Darby* (St. Louis: Hawthorn Publishing Company, [1978?]), 8.
8. Ibid., 12–13.
9. Jesse Benton Fremont, *Souvenirs of My Time* (Boston: D. Lothrop and Co., 1887), 66–67.
10. Ibid., 66.
11. *Personal Recollections of John F. Darby*, 41–43.
12. Charles Dickens, *American Notes* (New York: St. Martin's Press, 1985), 158.
13. Ibid., 158–159.
14. John Y. Simon, editor, *The Personal Memoirs of Julia Dent Grant (Mrs. Ulysses S. Grant)* (Carbondale and Edwardsville: Southern Illinois University Press), 55–56.
15. Ibid., 37.
16. Francis Parkman Jr., *The California and Oregon Trail* (New York: Hurst and Company), 7.
17. *Personal Memoirs of Julia Dent Grant*, 55–56.
18. "A Street Sketch," *St. Louis Post-Dispatch*, October 16, 1880, 4.
19. J. A. Dacus, Ph.D., and James W. Buel, *A Tour of St. Louis; or, the Inside Life of a Great City* (St. Louis: Western Publishing Company, 1878), 436.
20. Edward King, *The Great South: A Record of Journeys* (Hartford: American Publishing Company, 1875), 223.
21. "Denizens of Hop Alley Hide from Taker of Census," *St. Louis Post-Dispatch*, April 27, 1910.
22. The Realty Record and Builder, *Facts about St. Louis*, ed. St. Louis Architectural Club, May 1911, 4.

23. "Polanders Police St. Louis' Polish Quarter," *St. Louis Post-Dispatch*, September 25, 1902.
24. N. B. Young, editor, *Your St. Louis and Mine* (St. Louis: N. B. Young, 1937), 75.
25. Sara Teasdale, *Flame & Shadow* (New York: The MacMillan Company, 1925).
26. Interview with Billie Baudissin, April 28, 1987.
27. Interview with Bill Dunphy, August 1, 1997.
28. Interview with Frank Lafser, November 5, 1986.
29. Tennessee Williams, *Memoirs* (Garden City, N.Y.: Doubleday, 1972), 46.
30. *St. Louis Star-Times*, February 3, 1944.
31. "A Real Service Man's Town," *St. Louis Post-Dispatch*, April 17, 1943, reprinted from the *Philadelphia Record*.
32. "City Waits for Official Word to Celebrate," *St. Louis Post-Dispatch*, May 7, 1945.
33. "City Celebrates on Reports from Tokyo in Advance of Official Word," *St. Louis Post-Dispatch*, August 14, 1945.
34. Robert L. Burns, "The Bench Warmer," *St. Louis Globe-Democrat*, October 26, 1954.
35. Interview with Glenn Changar, March 12, 2015.
36. Ibid.
37. Obituary of Oscar Ozarowski, *St. Louis Post-Dispatch*, March 23, 2010.
38. Robert Paul Jordan, "A New Spirit Soars in Mid-America's Proud Old City St. Louis," *National Geographic*, 605.
39. Interview with Billie Baudissin, September 5, 1985.
40. Howard F. Baer, *Saint Louis to Me* (St. Louis: Hawthorn Publishing Company, 1978), 14.
41. Ibid., 14–15.
42. "Dynamite Considered at Height of Firestorm," *St. Louis Post-Dispatch*, April 4, 1976.
43. Jason Rosenbaum, "Historic Tax Credit Sparked 'Wildfire' of Development Downtown—and in Missouri," *St. Louis Beacon*, July 8, 2013.
44. Martin van der Werf, "Jerry Schlichter Thinks St. Louis Can Be Comeback City of the Country," *St. Louis Post-Dispatch*, July 8, 2005.
45. Dustin Bopp interview with NiNi Harris, March 31 2015.

# PHOTO CREDITS

(All other images are believed to be in the public domain.)

Jim Bailey: 132 bottom

City Museum: 136 upper left, 136 lower right

Culinaria: 130

William Greenblatt Photography LLC: 128

NiNi Harris personal collection: 26–27 f, 30, 46–47 i

Gail Keller: 133 upper left

Don Korte: ii, iv, v top, v bottom, 1, 3 top, 3 bottom, 6, 7 bottom, 26-27 a, 26-27 c, 52, 63, 70 top, 70 bottom, 74 top, 75 middle, 77, 106, 116 left, 119 bottom, 124 top, 125 bottom, 126 top, 126 middle, 131 left, 131 bottom right, 132 top, 132 middle, 133 middle left, 133 bottom, 135, 137, 138, 139, 142–143 b, 142–143 d, 142–143 f, 142–143 g, 142–143 h, 144, 146, 147, 152

Terry Lay, Visual Manager, Famous-Barr (retired): 114 top

Library of Congress: 32 top, 37, 50–51, 53 middle left, 53 lower left, 56–57, 65, 68 top, 68 bottom, 71, 74 bottom, 80–81 a, 85 top, 92 top

Lipic's Engagement: 110–111 a

Missouri Athletic Club: 76, 76–77

Missouri History Museum: vi, viii, 2 top, 2 bottom, 4-5, 7 top, 8-9, 10, 12 top, 12 middle, 13, 14, 15, 16–17, 18 top, 18 middle, 19, 20, 21, 22, 23, 24–25, 26–27 b, 26–27 d, 26–27 e, 28, 31 top, 31 bottom, 32 bottom, 33 top, 33 bottom, 34–35, 36 top, 36 bottom, 38 top, 38 bottom, 39, 40, 41 bottom, 42, 44–45, 46–47 a, 46–47 b, 46–47 c, 46–47 d, 46–47 e, 46–47 g, 46–47 j, 48, 53 upper left, 53 upper right, 53 lower right, 55 top, 55 middle, 55 bottom, 56 bottom, 57, 58, 59, 60, 61, 62 bottom, 64 top, 64 bottom, 66–67, 67, 69 top, 69 middle, 69 bottom, 72–73, 75 bottom, 78–79, 80–81 b, 80–81 c, 80–81 d, 80–81 e, 80–81 f, 83, 84, 85 bottom, 86–87, 88 top, 88 bottom, 89, 90 top, 90 bottom, 91, 92 bottom, 93, 94, 95, 96, 97, 98 top, 98 middle, 99, 100–101, 102, 103, 104–105, 108–109, 110–111 b, 110–111 c, 110–111 d, 110–111 e, 112, 115, 120 bottom, 122, 123, 140–141, 142–143 a, 142–143 c, 142–143 e

Tom Nagel/CityArchRiver Foundation: 134 upper right, 134 lower left, 134 lower right

Robert Pauly, Historian/Curator, St. Louis Fire Department: 129 insert

St. Louis Mercantile Library at University of Missouri–St. Louis: 43, 62 top, 116 right, 118 top, 119 top, 120 top, 125 top, 129

State Historical Society of Missouri–St. Louis: 107, 114 middle, 117 top, 117 bottom, 118 bottom, 121, 124 bottom, 127 top, 127 bottom

Studio X/Great Rivers Greenway: 134 upper left

# INDEX

(Italic page numbers indicate illustrations.)

1010 Pine building, 85, 124–125
Aloe Plaza, 108–109
Ambassador Theatre, 91, 91
Ambassadorables, 91
American Institute of Architects national convention, 63
Arcade Building, 130
Armistice Day parade, 104–105
Army Corps of Engineers, 6
Ashley tenement, 71, 74
Baer, Howard F., 123
Baileys' Range, 132
Baker's Shoes, 118
Bankers Lofts, 133
Baudissin, Billie, 89–91, 122
Beaugenou family, 18
Becker, August, 10
Bee Hat Building, 75
Benton, Thomas Hart, 31
Big Mound, 24–25
Billon, Frederic, 16–17
Boatmen's Tower, 124, 140
Boehl, Emil, 20
Boggs, Julia, 42
bond issue (1923), 84–85
Bopp, Dustin, 133
Bridge, Beach & Company, 2
Broadway (in 1858), 44–45
Brown, Joe E., 107
Brown Shoe, 69
Buchbleter, Eva, 117
Buel, James W., 51
Busch, Gussie, 123
Campbell, Robert, 38
Campbell, Virginia, 56, 56
Centenary Methodist Church, 74, 119
Changar, Henry, 113, 115
Changar, Shirley, 113, 115
Charless, Joseph, 20

Chemical Building, 110–111
Chinatown. See Hop Alley
Chouteau, Auguste, 10, 11, 12, 12
    residence of, 26–27
Chouteau, Major Pierre, 32
Chouteau's Mill, 19
Chouteau's Pond, 19, 26–27
Christ Church Cathedral, 90, 107
City Museum, 136
CityArchRiver, 135, 137, 138
Citygarden, 135, 138
Civil Courts Building, 93, 94, 95
Civil War, 40
Clark, William, 33
Cleveland, President and Mrs. Grover, 55
Consolidated Garment Company, 88
Culinaria, 130
Cupples Station warehouses, 52, 54, 131–132, 132, 142–143
Dacus, J. A., 51
Darby, John, 29
Darby, Mayor John, 29
De Finiels, Nicolas, 13, 14
Dent, Colonel Frederick, 42
Dent, Nellie, 42
Dickens, Charles, 34, 37, 37
Dolph Building, 91
Dunphy, Bill, 91
Eads Bridge, 31, 46–47, 50–51, 50–52, 52, 53, 54
Eads, James B., 51, 53
Easterly, Thomas, 26–27
Easton, Rufus, 20
Edison Brothers Shoes, 122
Edison Brothers Stores Building, 125, 125
Emerson Electric building, 98, 102, 130
Equitable Building, 124
Famous, 80–81
Famous-Barr department store, 114, 114–115
Fashion Square Building, 7, 88, 131

148

Federal Building, 9, 89, 102
Federal Court and Custom House, 50, 56, 57, 88, 93
federal customhouse, 32
Feeney, James, *107*, 107
Feeney's, 107
Fifth Street, corner of Washington Avenue, *58*
fire (1849), 35, *38*, 38
fire (1976), *128*, 128, 129
First Presbyterian Church, 49
flatboatmen, *13*, 26–27
Flint, Timothy, 21, 22
Flying Saucer Draught Emporium, *142–143*
Forshaw, Joseph, 76
Fourth Street
    corner of Olive Street (1848), *46–47*
    in front of Old Courthouse, *59*
Fowler, Charles, *110–111*
"Frankie and Johnnie," 74
Franklin Fire Company No. 8, *46–47*
Fremont, Jessie Benton, *31*, 31
Fremont, John C., 31, 35
French and Indian War, 15
Fritz, Wainwright & Co., *46–47*
Fur Exchange Building, 131
garment industry, 102, 116–117, *131*
Gast, Leopold, *38*
Gateway Arch, 9, 115–116, *120*, 120–123, *121*, *122*, *123*, *124*, *134*, 135, 137–138, *140-141*
Gateway Foundation, 138
Gateway Mall, 135, *142–143*
Gateway Tower, 124, 140
Grand Army of the Republic, 54
Grand Leader Building, *69*
Grant, Julia Dent, 42
Grant, Ulysses S., 42, 56
    residence of, *42*
Great Depression, 92, 97, 98
Great Rivers Greenway, *134*

Halstedt, Culver, 76
"Harlem Rag," 74
Hastings, Matthew, *33*, *46–47*
Hellmuth, Obata & Kassabaum, 124–125
Hop Alley, *61*, 61
International Shoe Company, 96, 102
Ittner, William B., 76
Jefferson National Expansion Memorial, 96, 115–116, 120–123, *134*
Jefferson, Thomas, 18
Johnson, Philip, 124
Jordan, Robert Paul, 119–120
Kamprad, Charles R., 128
Kargau, Ernst, 39
Keckley, Elizabeth, 33
Kiel Auditorium, *92*, 103
Kiener, Harry, 76
Kiener Plaza, 137
King, Edward, 54
Knickerbocker Building, *131*, 131–132
La Petite Riviere, *19*, 20
Labor Day parade, *100–101*
Laclede Gas Building, 124
Laclede Gas Light Company Building, 74
Laclede, Pierre, 10, 11, *12*, 12, 14, *26–27*
Laclede's Landing, 7, 126
Ladies' Auxiliary No. 66, United Automobile Workers, *100–101*
Lafayette, General, *32*, 32, 34
Lafitte, Jean, 33
Lafser, Frank, 91
Laurel, The, *142–143*
Law Library, *3*
Law Library Association, 3
Lindbergh, Charles, *90*, 90–91
Lindenwood University, 131
Link, Theodore, 64
Lipic's, *110–111*
log cabins, 18, 20, 29

Louis XV, 11
Louisiana Purchase, 18, 115
Lucas Grove, 38
Lucas Park, 56
Lucas Place, 38, 40, 49, 54, 56
Luther Ely Smith Park, 134
Majestic Stove Factory, 7
Mandan Indian village, 23
Manikowski, Michael, 74
Mansion House, 120, 124, 124, 125, 140
map of St. Louis (1804), 16–17
map of St. Louis (1849), 38
market house, 21
Mart Building, 102, 105
*Meeting of the Waters*, 108–109
Memorial Plaza, 2, 92–96, 108–109, 120
Mercantile Library, 46–47, 96
Merchandise Mart, 117, 130
Merchants Laclede Building, 131
Metropolitan Square Building, 125
Meyer, Marie, 110–111
Mill Creek, 20
Miller, Mayor Victor, 90, 93, 94
Milles, Carl, 108–109
Milles fountain, 108–109, 118
Miss Downtown St. Louis, 117, 127
Miss Hulling's Cafeteria, 142–143
*Mississippi* (steamer), 56–57
Missouri Athletic Club, 76, 76–77
Missouri Pacific Building, 85
Missouri Park, 55, 56
Modern Jacket Company, 117
Monroe School, 90
Monsanto Run to the Arch (1973), 127
Morton D. May Amphitheater, 142–143
Municipal Auditorium, 92, 92–93, 93, 105
Municipal Courts Building, 93
National Democratic Convention, 54, 55
National Electric Light Association, 54
National Suffrage Day, 80–81
Native Americans, 2, 12, 15, 21, 22, 31, 34
Old Cathedral, 33
Old Courthouse, 10, 46–47, 59, 124, 127, 134, 137
Old Post Office, 6, 56, 57, 88, 89, 107, 126, 126, 130–131
Old Post Office Square, 130–131, 135
Olive Street
    corner of Fourth Street (1848), 46–47
    corner of Third Street (1842), 33
    southeast corner of Seventh Street (1859), 41
One Bell Center, 124–125
Osage Indians, 12
Ozarowski, Oscar, 116–117
Park Avenue Coffee, 132
Parkman, Francis, 41, 41
Paul Brown Building, 88, 89, 130, 132
Peabody Opera House, 92
Pet Milk Building, 131
*Pike* (riverboat), 30
Planter's House, 34
Plaza Square Apartments, 119, 119, 120

Pollock Clothing Company, 88
Pollock, Rose, 88
Pollock, Sam, 88
population of St. Louis, 15, 30, 32–33, 35, 40, 65
post office, 26-27, 93
Pratte, Bernard, 42
Prizefighters' Row, 61
Raeder Building, 126, 126
Railway Exchange Building, 110–111, 133
Railway Lofts, 133
Rizzo, Thomas, 110–111
Robert Campbell House, 131
Roosevelt, President Franklin Delano, 92, 102
Roosevelt, President Theodore, 56–57
Rosebud Cafe, 74
Roth, Jacob, 32
Roy, Antoine, 20
Roy's Tower, 20, 23, 32
Saarinen, Eero, 115
Saengerbund, 54
St. John the Apostle Church, 74, 107
St. John the Baptist Church, 119
St. Louis Army Medical Depot, 102, 105
St. Louis Cardinals, 89–90, 123
St. Louis Carriage Company, 139
St. Louis City Hall, 65, 68, 68, 75, 86–87, 93
St. Louis Exposition Hall, 54, 55, 56, 65
St. Louis levee, 43, 46–47
St. Louis Public Library, Central Branch, 6, 70, 70, 75, 93
St. Louis University, 34, 59, 131
    "College Church," 36
St. Nicholas Hotel, 62, 63
St. Patrick's Day parade, 9
Saugrain, Dr. Antoine, 18
Schlichter, Jerry, 126, 130
Schotten, Christian, 39
Schotten, William, 39
Second Presbyterian Church, 49
Sedlak, Josef, 92
Seventh Street
    southeast corner of Olive Street (1859), 41
Shepard School, 90
Sherman, General William Tecumseh, 56
Skid Row, 61
Slide the City, 137
Smith, Luther Ely, 96, 96, 98
Smith, Private Edward J., 105
Smith, Sid, 42
Soldiers' Memorial, 8–9, 84–85, 85, 93, 106
Southwestern Bell, 85
Southwestern Bell Building payment window, 75
Stauss, Louis, 128
Stifel, Nicolaus & Co. building, 125, 125
Stix, Baer and Fuller department store, 69, 112, 113, 115, 115, 142–143
Stoddard, Captain Amos, 20
Stone, Edward Durell, 7, 123
Stouffer's Restaurant, 140
street illuminations, vi
street paving, 80–81

Sullivan, Louis, 3, 6, 60, 62, 63, 85
Sverdrup, Jack, 123
Syndicate Trust Building, 130, 132
Taft, William Howard, 71
Teasdale, Sarah, 83
Terminal Railroad Association, 65
Third Street
    corner of Olive Street (1842), *33*
Thomas F. Eagleton United States Courthouse, *142–143*
Tobin, Edward L., 61
Tony Faust's Cafe and Oyster Bar, *46–47*, *80–81*
Turpin, Tom, 74
Union Fire Company No. 2, *46-47*
Union Market, *110–111*, 131
Union Station, 7, 63-65, *64*, *65*, 75, 92, *103*, 105, *117*, *118*, 126, *152*
    coffee shop, *102*
Union Trust Building, 61, 63
United Service Organization (USO), 103, 105
Upper Louisiana, 15
Verandah Row, *46–47*
Von Phul, Anna Maria, *14*, *24–25*, *26–27*
Wainwright Building, 3, 6, 59-60, *60*, 63, *63*, 85
Walker, Sarah, 42
Wardenski, Stanislaus, 74
warehouse district, *80–81*
Warren, A. C., 31
Washington Avenue, 52, 59, 68, *69*, 70, 85, 88, *116–117*
    near Fifth Street, *58*
Washington Avenue Post, 132
Washington University, 34
    Collegiate Hall, *36*
Webster University, 131
*Wedding of the Rivers*, *108–109*
Wiggins Ferry Company, 30, 43
Wilcox, Lieutenant Cadmus, 42
Wild, John Caspar, *34–35*
Williams, Tennessee, 96
Wimar, Carl, 10
Works Progress Administration (WPA), *26–27*, 92, 98
World War I, 84
World War II, 98, 99, *102–107*
Wright Building, 130
Wyoming (steamer), *20*